on track ...

Duran Duran

every album, every song

Karen Windle

SONICBOND

sonicbondpublishing.com

Sonicbond Publishing Limited
www.sonicbondpublishing.co.uk
Email: info@sonicbondpublishing.co.uk

First Published in the United Kingdom 2025
First Published in the United States 2025

British Library Cataloguing in Publication Data:
A Catalogue record for this book is available from the British Library

ISBN 978-1-78952-368-3

Typeset in ITC Garamond Std & ITC Avant Garde Gothic

Graphic design and typesetting: Full Moon Media

Follow us on social media:
Twitter: https://twitter.com/SonicbondP
Instagram: www.instagram.com/sonicbondpublishing_/
Facebook: www.facebook.com/SonicbondPublishing/

Linktree QR code:

on track ...

Duran Duran

every album, every song

Karen Windle

SONICBOND

sonicbondpublishing.com

Would you like to write for Sonicbond Publishing?

We are mainly a music publisher, but we also occasionally publish in other genres including film and television. At Sonicbond Publishing we are always on the look-out for authors, particularly for our two main series, On Track and Decades.

Mixing fact with in depth analysis, the On Track series examines the entire recorded work of a particular musical artist or group. All genres are considered from easy listening and jazz to 60s soul to 90s pop, via rock and metal.

The Decades series singles out a particular decade in an artist or group's history and focuses on that decade in more detail than may be allowed in the On Track series.

While professional writing experience would, of course, be an advantage, the most important qualification is to have real enthusiasm and knowledge of your subject. First-time authors are welcomed, but the ability to write well in English is essential.

Sonicbond Publishing has distribution throughout Europe and North America, and all our books are also published in E-book form. Authors will be paid a royalty based on sales of their book. Further details about our books are available from www.sonicbondpublishing.com. To contact us, complete the contact form there or email info@sonicbondpublishing.co.uk

Dedication

This book is dedicated to my husband, Christopher Windle, whose endless support and patience (and photography skills) helped make this project possible, as well as to the memory of our beloved cat, Baby.

Thank you to Karen Mason-Blair for the wonderful photo of the band and the kind words, author Darren Johnson for the advice and members of the Duran Duran Message Board, past and present, for being a fount of knowledge about our favourite band on planet Earth. I'm also grateful to my family and friends for their supportive words and general excitement about this project, and to my cats, Mina and Dotty, who have been at my side during the entire writing process. I would also like to thank Stephen Lambe of Sonicbond Publishing for giving me the opportunity to write this book and, of course, the members of Duran Duran, who continue to inspire so many with their music, which helps make the world a more extraordinary place.

on track ...
Duran Duran

Contents

Introduction

Duran Duran formed in Birmingham, England, in 1978 and rose to dizzying heights of fame in the 1980s as the 'Fab Five'. Following their peak during that decade, they experienced lineup changes before their extraordinary comeback in 1993. The band, featuring the classic lineup, reunited in 2001 and have shown remarkable endurance since then, with four original members still on board. Duran Duran have released 16 studio albums and were inducted into the Rock & Roll Hall of Fame in 2022.

Founding members Nick Rhodes (born Nicholas Bates) and Nigel John Taylor – both raised in Hollywood, south Birmingham – met as pre-teens and instantly bonded over their shared musical tastes. The two were fans of glam rock acts like David Bowie and Roxy Music but were also inspired by the disco grooves of Chic and the punk ethos of The Sex Pistols. That mix of musical influences culminated in the formation of the band, which was rounded out by Stephen 'Tin Tin' Duffy, an art school chum of Taylor's and later a successful musical artist in his own right. Taylor's decision to attend art school at Birmingham Polytechnic, which was later renamed Birmingham City University, was inspired by his musical idols who had also studied art, including John Lennon and Roxy Music's Bryan Ferry.

Rhodes and Taylor had a keen interest in films and culled their fledgling band's namesake from the cult science-fiction flick *Barbarella*. They found their moniker in the name of the movie's mad scientist, Dr. Durand Durand, which they changed to Duran Duran.

The band made their live debut in 1979 with Duffy on bass guitar and vocals, Rhodes on synthesisers and tapes and Taylor on guitar. Simon Colley then joined on clarinet and bass, but both he and Duffy soon quit.

Taylor and Rhodes, seeking to become a five-piece act, added vocalist Andy Wickett, as well as drummer and fellow Brummie Roger Taylor. (Demos from Wickett's time in the group included an early version of 'Girls On Film'.) After John Taylor switched to bass and Alan Curtis briefly joined on guitar, Wickett also exited the band. Singer Jeff Thomas then had his own brief stint as part of the group.

During this time, Duran Duran began rehearsing at the Rum Runner in Birmingham, where they met the nightclub's owners (and future band managers), Paul and Michael Berrow. The band members honed their craft at the Rum Runner and even took on jobs at the venue. John Taylor worked the doors, Roger Taylor bused tables and Rhodes, fittingly, was a disc jockey.

After Curtis left and Thomas was let go, the band placed an ad in *Melody Maker* seeking a guitarist and found yet another unrelated Taylor. With the addition of Andy Taylor, originally from Tynemouth, followed by Hertfordshire-born vocalist Simon Le Bon, the classic lineup was complete. Le Bon – recommended for the role by a former girlfriend who was a barmaid at the Rum Runner – made a lasting first impression with his storied book of lyrics and pink leopard-print trousers. The band commenced rehearsals and wrote the song 'Sound Of Thunder' right out of the gate.

The new and improved five-piece made their live debut at the Rum Runner in July 1980. During this time, the band had become aligned with the New Romantic movement. Kahn & Bell, Birmingham designers who were hugely influential in the scene, dressed them for early performances and later provided clothing for the 'Planet Earth' video. Meanwhile, *Sounds* magazine printed the first UK article about the band, which introduced them as New Romantics.

In 1980, Michael Berrow mortgaged his house for the money to secure a high-profile opening slot on performer Hazel O'Connor's UK tour. Those shows sparked widespread interest in the band, which helped ignite a bidding war between EMI Records and Phonogram. By the end of the year – and at the urging of Dave Ambrose, the A&R director who had also signed The Sex Pistols – they inked a major-label recording contract with EMI.

More than four decades later, Duran Duran continue to record new music and tour regularly. They have expanded their fan base, thanks in part to the many musical artists who have cited them as an influence, including Beck, The Dandy Warhols, The Killers, Lady Gaga, No Doubt and Mark Ronson. Perhaps the key to their endurance is that they have retained a songwriting democracy, splitting their royalties among all official members.

Duran Duran rose to prominence during the age of music television – the ideal showcase for five 'pretty boys' in makeup and dressed in the latest fashions. As Le Bon told *Entertainment Weekly* in 2004, 'We came in, we seized our opportunity and we drove the band right into people's living rooms.'

However, their music was just as indelible as their music videos. From 'Hungry Like The Wolf' and 'Ordinary World' to 'Invisible' and beyond, they have had an enormous impact on popular culture and rightfully gained respect in the music industry.

Duran Duran (1981)

Personnel:
Simon Le Bon: vocals
Nick Rhodes: keyboards, synthesisers
Andy Taylor: guitars
John Taylor: bass
Roger Taylor: drums
Recorded at Red Bus Studios, Utopia Studios and Chipping Norton Recording Studios from December 1980 to January 1981
Produced by Colin Thurston
Engineer: Colin Thurston
Record label: EMI/Harvest/Capitol
Release date: June 1981
Highest chart places: UK: 3, US: 10
Running time: 39:42
Current edition: 2024 Warner Music CD/LP

The band's eponymous debut album introduced Duran Duran to the world as New Romantics, which – like most labels – was mainly convenient for marketing purposes. They had cut their teeth as a live act at Barbarella's, a nightclub that was part of the New Romantic scene in Birmingham and was coined after the film from which the band had also found a name. However, the assorted musical artists categorised as New Romantics, aside from sharing a love of glam rock and a penchant for ruffles and other similar fashion statements, were often quite musically different. In fact, the scene didn't even have a name until around the time that Duran Duran had emerged, seemingly fully formed, in the autumn of 1980.

Duran Duran mixed glam rock and disco, while bands like Spandau Ballet were heavily influenced by blue-eyed soul music. Other associated acts, such as Visage – whose original members included New Romantic tastemakers Steve Strange, Midge Ure and Rusty Egan, a DJ at The Blitz, the seminal London club – were inspired by pioneering German electronic band Kraftwerk. Ultravox (of which Ure was also a member) didn't even embrace New Romantic fashions. Japan, who were clearly influential on the scene, were often lumped into it but had no direct connection to it. Former punks Adam and the Ants, as well as Culture Club – likely the poppiest of the bunch – also scored chart success under the New Romantic banner. In modern music, the movement's name has had staying power, even inspiring the title of a song by pop mega-star Taylor Swift.

At the peak of New Romanticism, a bit of a friendly competition developed between the two biggest bands identified as part of the scene: Duran Duran, proud Brummies and the house band at the Rum Runner, and Spandau Ballet, a house band at The Blitz. This rivalry, fuelled in part by the press, pitted two five-piece groups of attractive, well-dressed men against one another. In the autumn of 1980, Duran Duran had only finished writing their first batch of songs. Yet, Spandau Ballet one-upped them by releasing their debut single, 'To Cut A Long Story Short', which hit the top five on the UK charts. Duran Duran's 'Planet Earth' followed in February 1981 but only reached number 12. Later, the two bands faced off on the BBC's *Pop Quiz*. (Duran Duran won the 1984 showdown.) As Spandau Ballet bassist Martin Kemp told *NME* in 2020:

> I was always proud of the fact that Spandau and Duran Duran were like Oasis and Blur or The Beatles and The Rolling Stones – where you pick two bands of a generation and you're either on one side or the other ... We were ridiculously competitive. Whatever they did, we tried to beat – and vice versa. To the point that it wasn't just about what number we were at in the charts; it was about how much money we'd spent on our recently completely overpriced videos and which location we went to film them. Even to the point where we were once at a party and the competition pathetically turned into who could stay up the latest. Whenever we met the boys, it was only friendly – and still is.

Duran Duran, armed with Le Bon's book of lyrics and aided by the songwriting chops of Andy Taylor, whose experience touring with cover bands proved valuable, had written all the songs for their debut album by the time they entered the studio. After signing with EMI, the band enlisted producer Colin Thurston to record *Duran Duran* in London and Oxfordshire. Thurston had impressive credentials, having served as a co-engineer and co-producer for Bowie and fellow glam rock hero Iggy Pop, as well as producing *Reproduction*, the first album by synth pop act The Human League. He proved to be the perfect producer for Duran Duran, helming their first album and their follow-up effort, *Rio*.

In a rare interview, with *Home & Studio Recording* in 1985, Thurston described hearing 'Girls On Film', the first song on the band's demo tapes: 'That was it. I didn't need to hear any more', he said. 'We went to Red Bus Studios, got the drum sound in 15 minutes, and in two weeks, we had the whole album done apart from the vocals.'

The album artwork features graphics by Malcolm Garrett of Assorted iMaGes – who also designed record sleeves for Buzzcocks, Simple Minds and others – which enhance a cover shot of the band photographed by Fin Costello. The members, dressed in the height of New Romantic fashion, pose: Le Bon, his face cast in shadow, leans on a vintage car, surrounded by Andy Taylor, bleach-blonde and sullen; Rhodes, hair dyed black and wearing a burgundy ascot; John Taylor, lurking in the back with his arms crossed; and Roger Taylor, with his hands in the pockets of his leather trousers.

What was truly remarkable about *Duran Duran*, in addition to the quality of the band's songwriting and playing, was the limited number of personnel involved in its making. Only the five band members and Thurston, who also engineered the album, are credited – no guest musicians. Duran Duran also used a similar approach when recording *Rio*, their seminal work.

'Girls On Film' (Duran Duran)
Released as a single in July 1981. Chart place: UK: 5
The sound of a clicking camera opens one of the band's most recognisable musical – and visual – moments. The band and their managers were keen to capitalise on the fast-growing art form of the music video, and the timing of their efforts was impeccable. The video for Duran Duran's third single was conceptualised with nightclubs in mind but ended up being released just as MTV launched in the US. In the clip, Duran Duran perform on a side stage as the real action takes place in a 'boxing ring', where topless women engage in pillow fights and other racy scenes, one even squaring off with a sumo wrestler. An uncensored version of the video, directed by Godley & Creme (of 10cc), proved to be popular in nightclubs with video screens, but only an edited version was permitted to air on MTV.

'Girls On Film' epitomised the disco-meets-post-punk aesthetic that the band had been aiming for. The song's catchy lyrics, slashing guitar riffs and strings played on a Crumar Performer (the sexy video didn't hurt either) catapulted the single to the UK top five – the band's highest chart place in their home country at the time – and a play on the song's title inspired many a newspaper headline writer over the years ('Boys On Film', etc.).

'Planet Earth' (Duran Duran)
Released as a single in February 1981. Chart place: UK: 12
Duran Duran's opening salvo of the New Romantic movement begins with the sound of Rhodes' Roland Jupiter-4 synth, processed by an MXR flanger, and really takes off with John Taylor's driving bassline. Strings – from the Crumar Performer and Jupiter-4 – line up behind the guitar for a tantalising combination. The song was released as the album's first single, with the 12" of the extended, remixed 'Night Version' bearing the message 'Duranies rock on' etched into the vinyl – what members of the band's growing fan base called themselves.

The single was accompanied by a video directed by Russell Mulcahy, soon to become a key collaborator of the band. The clip features the five members dressed in ruffled finery and two dancers who were friends of the band from the Rum Runner. The band members perform on what appears to be an icy ledge, which Le Bon jumps from into a seeming abyss at the clip's conclusion. To put the icing on the New Romantic cake, the song even includes a shout-out to the movement with the line 'like some New Romantic looking for the TV sound'. The track was very much of its moment yet featured music and lyrics – including the lines 'Look now, look all around. There's no sign of life' – that proved timeless, or perhaps futurist, a term associated with New

Romanticism and its embrace of a futuristic aesthetic that was often bandied about by Rhodes. Duran Duran made their first of many appearances on the BBC's *Top Of The Pops* to perform 'Planet Earth', a song which remains a touchstone for the band in terms of both their history and their live shows.

'Anyone Out There' (Duran Duran)

Duran Duran begins with two upbeat smash singles and barely slows down for one of the album's quieter moments. Taylor's guitar riffs are the key to keeping 'Anyone Out There' out of ballad territory. The juxtaposition of his rock-inflected guitar with Rhodes' ethereal synths (with another appearance from the Crumar Performer), which together open this track, always threatened to pull the band members in different musical directions but worked like a charm on their early efforts. Behind those opposing musical forces featured on this track and other early ones were John Taylor's more-than-proficient bass playing and Roger Taylor's ever-steady drumming, which imparted a four-on-the-floor rhythm inspired by Chic.

Le Bon croons wistfully throughout the song, which draws to its conclusion as he repeatedly asks, or perhaps just states, since there's no question mark in the title, 'Anyone out there?' backed with some slap bass from Taylor. It's a break-up song that's far from typical.

'To The Shore' (Duran Duran)

This darkly beautiful song, one of Rhodes' favourites on the album, wasn't included on the LP's US release, to which a newer single, 'Is There Something I Should Know?' was later added. But 'To The Shore' is far from a throwaway track. It's moody and explores darker themes often associated with New Romanticism, with some of Le Bon's most experimental lyrics yet, including the lines 'I'm moving Chrissie pretty flowers in the shutter maze'. The singer has said that the lyrics refer, in part, to a tutor at Birmingham University named Chrissie, whom he was fascinated with. Taylor's guitar riffs again provide the counterpoint to Rhodes' synthesiser work for that mix of rock and synth pop that the band soon became known for.

'Careless Memories' (Duran Duran)

Released as a single in April 1981. Chart place: UK: 37

The UK chart performance of the album's second single was a bit of a disappointment after 'Planet Earth' nearly hit the top ten. Le Bon again pines over a lost love, even casting aside a bouquet of flowers in an angrier moment from the music video, directed by Perry Haines.

Even before 'Girls On Film', Duran Duran were gaining attention for their compelling videos. The band members' on-screen presence was no doubt aided by the fact that they were five attractive, fashionably dressed guys who didn't shy away from wearing makeup. But it was also boosted by Le Bon's background in acting. He had studied drama at Birmingham University and even appeared in adverts as a child, and his expressive blue eyes and trademark pout were front and centre in 'Careless Memories', as in most of the band's other videos.

The decision to release 'Careless Memories' as the second single was EMI's choice, as the band favoured 'Girls On Film'. But time has been kind to this track, which was still a fine choice for a single because of its catchy music and lyrics, and has thus become a staple at their concerts. It's an evergreen break-up song set to a driving, danceable beat. Rhodes' swirling synths and Taylor's well-timed guitar licks dominate the track, which builds until Le Bon repeatedly shouts, 'Look out!' at its conclusion.

'Night Boat' (Duran Duran)

Side two of the album veers into darker but no less brilliant territory, beginning with 'Night Boat'. The song opens with Rhodes' eerie synths and Taylor's guitar stabs before Le Bon joins in for one of their most gothic moments. (Fittingly, the band, with Taylor back in the fold, re-recorded the song for their Halloween-themed album, *Danse Macabre*.) Rhodes and Taylor are opposing forces throughout the song, its music building in intensity as Le Bon begins waiting – here, for the night boat; later on the album, for the sound of thunder.

In the video, which appeared on the band's groundbreaking video album (aka 'The First 11 Videos'), the night boat is a ghostly ship teeming with zombie-like ghouls before zombies went mainstream in popular culture. Mulcahy directed the clip, which was filmed in 1982 in Antigua, along with the 'Rio' video. It opens with Le Bon as he reads from *Romeo And Juliet* before the horror and mayhem ensue.

'Sound Of Thunder' (Duran Duran)

The first song written by the classic lineup is arguably one of their best. The song opens with the pulsating sounds of Rhodes' synths – he used the Jupiter-4, the Crumar Performer and a Sequential Prophet-5 sequencer on the track – before Roger Taylor's drums kick in, capped by John Taylor's galloping bassline. Andy Taylor's guitar takes more of a back seat on the song, which gives way to a full-on disco breakdown at its midsection.

Le Bon's subject – a man who starts World War III, according to the singer – lies in the grass as he's left waiting for the sound of thunder. 'Here I am, I'm a dotted line', he sings. 'Cut the corners, stick me to your door. I'm the man who stepped off the path'. 'Sound Of Thunder' doesn't follow a conventional path for the band, who had offered mostly poppier moments on the album's A-side but were now showing a more serious, experimental side on the LP's second half.

'Friends Of Mine' (Duran Duran)

A song whose chorus references armed robber George Davis ('Georgie Davies' here) and a song performed by The Beatles ('No more heroes, we twist and shout') wouldn't be the most likely candidate to be a live staple. But Duranies can't help but dance and sing along to this spirited track – a rare non-single that became one of the band's trademark songs.

In the lyrics, Le Bon addresses people he thought were friends, but 'they were just wasting time. Out on the dotted line'. His use of 'dotted line' in back-to-back tracks seems to be less a lyrical touchstone than part of his tendency to write cryptically. This harder-edged track (for Duran Duran, at least) offers a perfect opportunity for Andy Taylor to rock out and for Le Bon's vocals to go from a whisper to a scream in a matter of lines. The song is quirky and borderline campy – quintessential Duran Duran.

A video, which shows the band performing and sitting around a table playing cards, has more in common with the promotional clips typical of the day than with their penchant for breaking new ground on film. In fact, the clip was filmed for television and never intended to be an official video.

'Tel Aviv' (Duran Duran)
Duran Duran's first attempt at an instrumental track didn't begin as such. The album version is synth-heavy and only features Le Bon as he wails seemingly imperceptible lyrics. But an early demo of the song harks back to 1970s heavy metal, with full lyrics, a booming bassline and guitar heroics galore.

The final track retains only the title from the original version, as live strings, Rhodes' Prophet-5 and Andy Taylor's Roland Guitar Synth combine to create layers of sound. Though uncredited in the liner notes, Richard Myhill arranged the strings.

Despite the edginess of the original 'Tel Aviv', it's hard to imagine Duran Duran as a straight-ahead rock band. The members, and perhaps Thurston, rightly steered this song (and 'Girls On Film', which also exists as an earlier, heavier AIR Studios demo) in a different direction. The two demos clearly show a band finding their footing, but *Duran Duran* displayed one that was fully formed.

Extra Tracks

'Late Bar' (Duran Duran)
The band's dark party anthem, the B-side of 'Planet Earth', evokes the image of 'things with legs' crawling through a hole in the wall during 'an all-night party in room 7609'. Andy Taylor's edgy guitar riffs open the track, on which John and Roger Taylor lock in for a danceable groove and Rhodes' synths wash over the proceedings. The track, which is about the Rum Runner, is nearly as catchy as the album's lead single and the perfect accompaniment to Le Bon's 1980 pronouncement in *Sounds*, 'We want to be the band to dance to when the bomb drops'.

'Khanada' (Duran Duran)
The B-side to 'Careless Memories' in the US and the UK features somewhat cryptic lyrics from Le Bon and music with a Middle Eastern flair. He sings, 'I

don't believe in dragons or blue. (Khanada I'll get by.) I don't believe in nobody's rules'. It's not a song that follows the path of a traditional pop song, either. It's all swirling synths, driving bass and crashing cymbals, building in intensity during the chorus and concluding with a sitar-infused outro.

Le Bon has said that he wrote the song about Jane Kahn of Kahn & Bell, the groundbreaking New Romantic fashion boutique in Birmingham. The label and their personal style were influenced by fantasy as well as Eastern cultures, so the song is a fitting tribute to the designer.

'Fame' (David Bowie, Carlos Alomar, John Lennon)

This cover of the Bowie classic about the troubles of fame accompanied 'Khanada' on the B-side of the UK single for 'Careless Memories'. Le Bon changes up the phrasing, and the band members step up the tempo for their version, their first of several Bowie covers. (In later years, they performed and/or recorded superb versions of 'Diamond Dogs', 'Boys Keep Swinging', 'Starman' and 'Five Years', as well as 'Fame' co-writer Lennon's 'Instant Karma!')

On 'Fame', as on most of their cover songs, they add their own touch with Rhodes' signature synth flair as well as Andy Taylor's interpretation of Alomar's brilliant guitar riff.

'Faster Than Light' (Duran Duran)

This pleasant tune that backs 'Girls On Film' is probably the fourth best of the album's B-sides. It still gives Le Bon a chance to do some vocal gymnastics and John Taylor to show off his chops on bass. Duran Duran named a tour after the song, which reflects the significance that every piece of music had in the band's earliest days.

If all four extra tracks had been included on *Duran Duran*, perhaps it could have been on its way to becoming a killer double album. The classic lineup had an abundance of quality material from the start – a testament to their songwriting talent.

Rio (1982)

Personnel:
Simon Le Bon: vocals, vibraphone, ocarina
Nick Rhodes: keyboards, synthesisers, sound effects, vocals
Andy Taylor: guitars, vocals
John Taylor: bass, vocals
Roger Taylor: drums, percussion
Additional musicians:
Andy Hamilton: saxophone
Recorded at AIR Studios, London, from January to March 1982
Produced by Colin Thurston
Engineer: Colin Thurston
Record label: EMI/Harvest/Capitol
Release date: May 1982
Highest chart places: UK: 2, US: 6
Running time: 42:38
Current edition: 2024 Warner Music CD/LP

If Duran Duran sought to make inroads in the music business with their first album, they aimed for the sky with their follow-up.

The band scored their first top-five hit in the UK with 'Girls On Film' but hadn't yet broken through in America. Yet, in 1982, the timing couldn't have been better for them. In the UK, the New Romantic movement turned out to be short-lived, but synth pop was in its heyday. In the US, radio stations like KROQ in Los Angeles and WLIR in New York were embracing new wave – a musical genre that stemmed from the punk scene in the UK as well as the CBGB era in New York City. New wave became a convenient catch-all term for slightly off-kilter bands that lacked a harder edge, such as Blondie and Talking Heads, which had been categorised as punk rock in the 1970s despite not entirely fitting into the genre. In the 1980s, new wave came to define not only these bands but also synth pop acts from the UK and elsewhere.

The East and West coasts of the US were the first to take notice of Duran Duran. In 1981, New York's WLIR became the first radio station in the country to play their music, after which the band embarked on their first headline tour of North America. Los Angeles' KROQ became another early supporter of the band.

Beyond the coasts, the fledgling music television channel MTV was expanding into cities and smaller towns across the country, exposing young music fans to what was fast becoming a Second British Invasion. At its start, MTV aired nothing but music videos, introduced by VJs, 24 hours a day. Many established radio stars were slow to catch on to the new art form or even dismissed it as a passing fad. Others simply provided makeshift videos of themselves performing live on a sound stage. UK acts spotted an opportunity that proved to be mutually beneficial for both them and MTV.

Duran Duran went a step further when their managers actually met with MTV executives about precisely the type of videos the channel sought. The result: a series of glossy travelogues that put the band on the map internationally.

The MTV execs laid out exactly what they wanted, John Taylor told *Billboard* magazine in 2014:

> 'Listen, you know, if we could have anything, we'd have videos that look like James Bond films.' And who better to interpret that [than] Russell [Mulcahy], who always thought like a feature film director? He always had the vision of a feature film director. We had an equal measure of grandiosity. But you know what, it was [the] right time at the time. The videos that we made in Sri Lanka ['Lonely In Your Nightmare', 'Hungry Like The Wolf' and 'Save A Prayer'] were game-changers. We know that.

In addition to working with Duran Duran on the 'Planet Earth' video, Mulcahy helmed The Buggles' seminal 'Video Killed The Radio Star'. He went on to direct a slew of videos for Duran Duran and others, including his groundbreaking clips from *Rio* up through the budget-busting video for 'The Wild Boys', before turning his attention to feature films.

As with *Duran Duran*, *Rio* featured artwork by Malcolm Garrett in addition to a painting commissioned by the band from American artist Patrick Nagel. Unlike the cover of their first LP, on which Garrett's graphics appear with an image of the band, the *Rio* artwork depicts a woman with an inviting 'cherry ice cream smile', which resulted in what's considered to be one of the most famous album covers of the 1980s. In 2024, the inspiration for the painting was finally revealed to have been a photo of model Marcie Hunt, which appeared in *Vogue Paris*.

A photo of the band, taken by Andy Earl, appears inside the album packaging. In it, the five members are posed on the roof of the British Petroleum HQ, which was then London's tallest building. They had shed their New Romantic look in favour of new wave skinny ties and Antony Price silk suits.

While the band's image and videos played an immense role in the success of *Rio*, the music was far from an afterthought. The band retained the pop sensibilities as well as some of the darker undertones heard on their debut album, yet took their music in a more escapist direction with songs (and videos) such as the title track and 'Hungry Like The Wolf'. Duran Duran worked with Thurston again, recording the album at AIR Studios, London. Paul McCartney was simultaneously recording his *Tug Of War* album at the studio, which had also been co-founded by legendary Beatles producer George Martin.

Initially released in May 1982, *Rio* was an instant smash in the UK. But it didn't make waves in the US until producer David Kershenbaum was hired to remix the album's A-side to make the songs more palatable to radio listeners in North America, resulting in more polished, rock-oriented mixes.

Yet, Duran Duran's desire to conquer America was there all along – in the title track itself.

'Rio' (Duran Duran)
Released as a single in November 1982. Chart places: UK: 9, US: 14
A song many believe is solely about a girl is also about America and the band's ambitions. Listeners wouldn't be wrong to assume that seemingly straightforward lyrics like 'Her name is Rio and she dances on the sand' would refer only to a woman. The indelible video – featuring a body-painted woman, played by model Reema Ruspoli – also plays into this trope. But listen further: the song is mainly about the US, 'from mountains in the north down to the Rio Grande'. Le Bon has confirmed this interpretation over the years, but the dual meaning helps give the song its universal appeal.

The video, directed by Mulcahy, features the band at play on a beach in Antigua. Released as a recession roiled the UK, the hugely popular clip furthered the band's association with the aspirational lifestyle, especially the unforgettable images of all five members on a yacht dressed in expensive Antony Price silk suits, which were famously ruined by saltwater. But the video – including humorous scenes featuring a pink telephone being served on a platter and Andy Taylor being thrown off-board the yacht – seems more tongue-in-cheek than anything.

However, it wasn't all fun in the sun: Simon Milne, an assistant to Mulcahy, recounted in *Melody Maker* in 1983 that the hard-working band members planned a brief holiday during their time in Antigua but abandoned those plans when shooting ran late and the now-classic video was captured.

Rhodes, in addition to keyboards and synths, is credited with 'sound effects' on the album, one of which opens the title track. He achieved the effect by tossing metal rods onto the strings of a grand piano and reversing the tape loop with producer Thurston's help. Background sounds fill out the song, giving it a Carnival feel. Thurston said that synthesised seagulls and other noises were added using a new Yamaha synth, which Rhodes was given to experiment with.

The track, which has roots in an earlier song performed by the band called 'See Me Repeat Me', was built on the rhythm section's groove, driven by John Taylor's syncopated bassline. With Rhodes' arpeggiated synths, Andy Taylor's flanged guitar and Le Bon's layers of lush harmonies, the members all conspire to produce a timeless track. The song also features a memorable sax solo by Andy Hamilton, the album's only guest musician. 'Rio', which was the album's final single, closes most of the band's concerts to this day.

'My Own Way' (Duran Duran)
Released as a single in November 1981. Chart place: UK: 14
An early version of 'My Own Way' was released as a single in the UK prior to the release of *Rio*. The track that appears on the album, the lyrics marked with the date 'May '81' inside the liner notes, features a slower tempo and a

rock edge, with a greater emphasis on Taylor's chunky guitar riffs. This rawer version, which lacked the original's 'disco strings', was deemed to fit best among the album's more exuberant tracks. The song is also notable for its shout-out to the former Peppermint Lounge in New York – '7UP between Sixth and Broadway' – which Duran Duran played on their first North American tour.

The colourful video, directed by Mulcahy, is a performance clip featuring a matador, played by actor Adrian Paul, and twirling flamenco dancers. Both the video and the song offered a burst of optimism that was welcome in the UK early in the decade. This cheerful, danceable track and *Rio* as a whole provided a sense of escapism for young people in the UK amid the recession and the Falklands War.

'Lonely In Your Nightmare' (Duran Duran)

This song, with its sweetly melancholy lyrics and a bassline reminiscent of Rick James' 'Super Freak', marked the band's first real foray into ballad territory. Le Bon pines for a woman, imploring her to 'let me in', albeit somewhat poetically. 'C'mon show me all the light and shade that made your name', he sings in lyrics, mixing subtlety and sexual longing as he continues, 'I know you've got it in your head, I've seen that look before'. Add in John Taylor's classic fretless bassline – which the band later acknowledged was similar to the one from James' r&b hit with the appearance of the mash-up 'Super Lonely Freak' on *Danse Macabre* – and the result is a unique ballad with a rather fast-paced drum pattern that works like a charm.

The video, which was directed by Mulcahy and filmed in Sri Lanka, features model Vanya Seager, who also appeared in the 'Save A Prayer' video. Black-and-white footage filmed in London, including close-up shots of each of the band members, was later added to the clip.

'Hungry Like The Wolf' (Duran Duran)

Released as a single in May 1982. Chart places: UK: 5, US: 5

The band's first big US hit was boosted by its classic video, in which Le Bon chases an animalistic woman, played by model Sheila Ming, through the streets of Sri Lanka and a jungle. Instead of being a James Bond pastiche, as MTV had requested, the video has a plot similar to an *Indiana Jones* film, with Le Bon wearing a fedora and running across a precarious footbridge over a body of water. The clip, directed by Mulcahy (who also provided the hat), was named one of the best music videos of all time by MTV and VH1. Along with 'Girls On Film', it was the first to win a Grammy Award for best short-form music video.

The song itself is just as iconic. The track was built around Rhodes' shimmering synths, produced by his new Roland Jupiter-8, and his girlfriend provided the laughter that opens the song. John Taylor's chugging bassline and Roger Taylor's drum fills play off Andy Taylor's edgy guitar riffs. Roger

Taylor's Simmons electronic kit, which he used on the album along with acoustic drums, achieves a dynamic, ambient sound also heard on other 1980s hits, including Phil Collins' 'In The Air Tonight'.

'Hungry Like The Wolf' is also lyrically strong and includes the LP's first subtle shout-out to singer Gordon Lightfoot, as Le Bon has stated that his famous 'do-do-do-dos' were inspired by the line 'What a tale your thoughts could tell' from the folk singer's 'If You Could Read My Mind'. The track, capped with a woman's moans, was an instant pop-rock classic and remains one of the band's most enduring hits. The single reached the top five in the UK and the US, the latter after the release of Kershenbaum's remix, in which the vocals and guitar are more prominent in the mix.

'Hold Back The Rain' (Duran Duran)

The lyrics of this song (dated '19th March '82' in the album liner notes) are about John Taylor, whose struggles with drinking and drugs during the 1980s and 1990s are now well-documented. After writing the lyrics, Le Bon stated on VH1's *Behind The Music* that he slipped a copy of them under Taylor's door. 'People tell me I haven't changed at all. But I don't feel the same,' Le Bon laments, 'and I bet you've had that feeling, too.' Later, he assures his bandmate, 'Okay, go off and wander. I'm guilty just the same. Sometimes you're needed badly. So please come back again'.

Rhodes' synths start the track before Le Bon launches into the heartfelt lyrics, accompanied by Taylor's galloping bassline, Andy Taylor's sharp guitar riffs and Roger Taylor's powerful drums.

This sentimental fan favourite, which exists in several different remixes and edits, is always a welcome addition to the live setlist.

'New Religion' (Duran Duran)

The song, dated '27th August '80' in the album liner notes, is described as 'a dialogue between the ego and the alter ego'. In it, the band members put on a musical display worthy of the song's profound nature. Le Bon, a self-described agnostic, delivers the scattered lyrics, seemingly about an internal struggle, in rapid-fire succession. Mentions of cross-carrying, church bells ringing and Army majors precede the line 'Searching for the undeniable truth that a man is just a fool'. Le Bon also plays vibraphone, and John and Roger Taylor lock in for a funky rhythm inspired by Bowie's 'Stay'. Andy Taylor delivers riffs that channel Pink Floyd's David Gilmour while also veering into funk territory with the rhythm guitar track, and Rhodes adds eerie synths, including from the Crumar Performer and the Prophet-5.

'Last Chance On The Stairway' (Duran Duran)

This effervescent track is one of Duran Duran's tenderest moments. The song, which opens with the sound of a cigarette being lit and Rhodes' atmospheric synth line, brings to mind a chance meeting at a party with both its lyrics and music. The rhythm section produce a delectable groove, and the synths sparkle throughout. The bridge features a marimba solo (which Rhodes has said he believes he played, though some sources credit Le Bon) before Andy Taylor's soaring guitar kicks in. It culminates with Le Bon as he croons, 'Wonder why ... (ooh-ooh-ooh) what makes me rise so high. Maybe it's something they put in your perfume or the look in your eyes'. The track is filled with longing and possibility, recalling being young during the 1980s at every turn, and it's a song that any hopeless romantic would never want to come to an end.

'Save A Prayer' (Duran Duran)
Released as a single in August 1982. Chart place: UK: 2
This wistful ballad is about what some people may call a one-night stand, but Duran Duran call it paradise. It was released in the UK as a single, which was accompanied by a video directed by Mulcahy and filmed in Sri Lanka. In it, the band members walk barefoot amid the ruins of a Buddhist temple. Other memorable scenes feature Rhodes and John Taylor atop an elephant and the band members perched in a tree. But capturing those scenes resulted in some scary moments for two of the Fab Five: an elephant ran away with Roger Taylor still on its back, and Andy Taylor fell into a lagoon and was subsequently hospitalised with malaria after he ingested some of the water.

The song features Rhodes' famous arpeggiated synth riff and lilting melody line, which he produced using a range of Roland gear – a CSQ-100 sequencer, an SH-2, his new Space Echo unit and the Jupiter-8. The track also features both electric and acoustic guitar, and the rhythm section take a back seat with an understated groove that reminds the listener more of Roxy Music than Chic. Le Bon takes centre stage with his anthemic lyrics and a melody again inspired by Lightfoot's 'If You Could Read My Mind'. The singer has stated that Lightfoot's line 'And you won't read that book again' inspired his own 'Don't save a prayer for me now' – though another 1980s smash, Whitney Houston's 'The Greatest Love Of All', bears a much more striking resemblance to the folk rock hit.

The mix of cutting-edge synths and classic balladry propelled 'Save A Prayer' to number two in the UK. In 1985, a version of the song from the live album *Arena* was released in the US, reaching number 16.

'The Chauffeur' (Duran Duran)
A song that's perhaps Duran Duran's crowning achievement is arty to its core. 'The Chauffeur' had its germination in 1978, during which time Le Bon worked on a kibbutz (a traditionally agriculture-based community) in Israel and nursed a crush on a female soldier he saw riding a tracker. Inspired in part by Bruce Springsteen's 'Born To Run', Le Bon moved the story about unrequited love from a desert setting to the futuristic 'tar plains'. The lyrics, including the memorable line 'Sing blue silver', have poetic elements that

evoke images such as aphids swarming 'up in the drifting haze'. In fact, the song originated with a poem written by Le Bon. In addition, the track is likely the best-known song to feature an extended ocarina solo, played by Le Bon, and includes a spoken-word sample from a nature record about insects.

'The Chauffeur' began as an acoustic track, but Rhodes (accompanied by Le Bon, as the main songwriter) took it in an electronic direction using a rhythm box, a sequencer and even the sound effect of ice cubes being dropped into water. He also helped Thurston mix the album, famously joining the band late for the shooting of their music videos in Sri Lanka.

The video is a world away from the colourful, action-packed clips directed by Mulcahy. 'The Chauffeur' is a black-and-white short film featuring three scantily clad women and an erotic dance. The clip, directed by Ian Emes, was the first not to include any band members, a departure for an act whose image was so key to their success. Instead of being influenced by the blockbuster movies of the day, it drew its inspiration from the work of photographer Helmut Newton, who was known for his black-and-white photos depicting racy subject matter.

The closing track of *Rio* was, in some ways, an artistic launching point for a band who, throughout their career, took chances, pushed creative boundaries and thus gained respect musically. But first, they were about to become princes of pop and teen idols whose level of success in the 1980s drew comparisons to Beatlemania.

As Roger Taylor said in the documentary *Classic Albums: Duran Duran – Rio*, 'We were in a period of time when everything we touched seemed to be turning to gold.'

Extra Tracks

'Like An Angel' (Duran Duran)

The single version of 'My Own Way' was backed with the superb B-side 'Like An Angel', and both songs also exist as earlier Manchester Square demos. In this romantic track in the vein of 'Last Chance On The Stairway', Le Bon pursues an angel, or perhaps just a woman who has 'eyes like an angel', with lines like 'Take your place among those twilight gleaming rivers that you read. Give me reasons to believe'. It features gentle guitar riffs from Andy Taylor and a whistled solo by Le Bon.

Seven And The Ragged Tiger (1983)

Personnel:
Simon Le Bon: vocals
Nick Rhodes: keyboards, synthesisers
Andy Taylor: guitars
John Taylor: bass
Roger Taylor: drums
Additional musicians:
Michelle Cobbs: vocals on 'The Reflex' and 'Union Of The Snake'
B. J. Nelson: vocals on 'The Reflex' and 'Union Of The Snake'
Raphael Dejesus: percussion
Mark Kennedy: percussion
Andy Hamilton: saxophone
Recorded at AIR Montserrat from April to October 1983
Produced by Alex Sadkin, Ian Little and Duran Duran
Engineers: Phil Thornalley and Peter Wade-Schwier
Record label: EMI/Capitol
Release date: November 1983
Highest chart places: UK: 1, US: 8
Running time: 37:36
Current edition: 2024 Warner Music CD/LP

Duran Duran, boosted by the rise of music television and appearances in teen magazines in the wake of *Rio*, were fast becoming one of the biggest pop bands in the UK and elsewhere. However, there's almost always a downside to success, and soon, their non-stop touring and promotional schedule, competing interests and even strife among some of the members and their managers began to weigh on the band. But first, Duran Duran were ready to present a united front with their third album, *Seven And The Ragged Tiger*, named for the five members and their two managers; the 'ragged tiger' being success.

After receiving a warm reception for *Rio*, the band packed a lot of other achievements into the mere year-and-a-half between albums. The band opened for Blondie in the US, playing ever-bigger venues. Capitalising on the success of their sophomore album, Capitol Records re-released *Duran Duran* in the US with a new track, 'Is There Something I Should Know?', which was a smash hit both there and in the UK. The band also broke ground with the release of the *Duran Duran* video album, featuring all 11 of their official videos up to and including the fresh hit 'Is There Something I Should Know?'.

Meanwhile, the appeal of each individual band member, both visually and personality-wise, was creating a teen sensation. Simon Le Bon was the dashing leading man, with his blue eyes and confident manner. John Taylor, who had once worn eyeglasses, was now a teen magazine pin-up with his handsome face, broad smile and introspective nature. Nick Rhodes – the mysterious, arty one, who at the age of 22 had already released a book of his photography titled *Interference* – was most often bleach-blonde and usually in a full face of makeup. Andy Taylor, as the 'bad boy' in the 'boy band' trope, gave the group their rock edge. Roger Taylor was the quiet yet handsome one. Never mind that they all had major musical chops, too.

Rhodes, who had taken a keen interest in the mixing process during *Rio* and helped co-produce Kajagoogoo's debut album, *White Feathers* – which included the UK number-one single 'Too Shy' – with Colin Thurston, played an outsize role in the musical direction of *Seven And The Ragged Tiger*. Excess marked the sessions for the album, which was officially recorded at AIR Montserrat in the Caribbean. At their managers' urging to avoid paying the UK's high tax rates, recording took place entirely outside their native country, including at a mobile studio in the south of France, and the album was mixed at Studios 301 in Sydney, Australia. The scattered recording process and lack of pre-written material resulted in an album which was well-timed for chart success but whose musical quality was uneven at points. Also during this time, the fatigue from non-stop work caught up with the band, John and Andy Taylor's use of drugs and alcohol escalated and Rhodes was hospitalised after suffering from an abnormally fast heartbeat.

Instead of working again with Thurston, the band employed Ian Little, who had co-produced 'Is There Something I Should Know?' with them. In Montserrat, they brought in Alex Sadkin, a producer for artists including Grace Jones, Robert Palmer and Thompson Twins. Before Thurston's death in 2007, the band had been in talks about going back into the studio with him, but *Rio* ended up being their last studio album with the producer who had played such a key role in their musical development.

The creation of the *Seven And The Ragged Tiger* album cover was also marked by excess. The band flew in an actual Bengal tiger for the photo shoot at the State Library of New South Wales in Sydney. The band members are dressed mostly in black formalwear in the photo (shot by Rebecca Blake), which adorns the cover along with the now-famous 'DD' logo, graphics by Malcolm Garrett that depict mystical-looking symbols and a map painted by Keith Breeden. The eye of the tiger (at the centre of one symbol) and a rectangular photo of its fur are the only traces of the animal featured on the final cover.

Individual band members flew in and out of the recording sessions for various commitments, and together, they played live sets at a charity concert at Villa Park in Birmingham as well as the Prince's Trust gala in London, where it was later revealed that Prince Charles and Princess Diana had been the target of a foiled assassination attempt by the Irish Republican Army. Also at the event, the band members famously met Diana, one of the most illustrious Duranies.

In 2007, Le Bon told the audience at the Concert for Diana, held to mark ten years since her passing, 'We are honoured that she always referred to Duran Duran as her favourite band, as she was certainly our favourite princess.'

The Princess of Wales was a popular public figure, at least with a good portion of the British populace, yet Duran Duran's public image was also becoming aligned with more divisive figures. To some, their glossy videos showing the band on yachts and in other exotic locales made them seem out of touch with many Britons who faced hardships during Margaret Thatcher's time as prime minister. But any attempt in the press to link them to Thatcherism was an unfair characterisation, according to Garrett, who played a key role in the band's branding. As he told *Louder Than War* in 2021:

> With Duran Duran, it was more like, 'Hey, we're selling you luxury goods', so I tried to think of it in terms of something more global, more international. I hate the word 'aspirational', but that was it ... I never saw it in quite those terms [Thatcherite]. Because Thatcher was really quite greedy and all about self, but if you talk to John and Nick, they're very generous people.

This view of the band and their status as teen idols who were only popular with young girls prompted a backlash in the music and tabloid press. *Seven And The Ragged Tiger* itself received mostly negative reviews upon its release. With critics like Paul Morley at *NME* fanning the flames with dismissive nicknames like 'Diana Diana', the resulting effects took years to overcome. As Roger Taylor told *The Palm Beach Post* in 2016, 'We put a lot into our albums, and I don't think we quite got the acclaim that we ought to from our records.'

In addition, it wasn't uncommon for mainstream publications to simultaneously praise and insult the band. In the wake of Duran Duran's third album, for example, *Rolling Stone* magazine officially proclaimed them 'The Fab Five' on its cover. But the article inside, by James Henke, was written in a fashion typically seen in media coverage of pop culture that appealed to young people in the 1980s. It focused heavily on Le Bon's non-existent weight problem and 'tortured singing' and dismissed the band's stage show as having a grandness that 'smacked of pretentiousness'. But the article – especially to someone reading it years later – clearly smacks of an attempt at knocking the band down a peg.

Ahead of the festive season, *Seven And The Ragged Tiger* was released and hit number one in the UK. That an album with several timeless tracks managed to come out of such a chaotic period and up against a Christmas deadline, no less, was a bit miraculous. Rhodes again helped mix the album, and Le Bon experienced 'writer's block', perhaps for the first time. The keyboardist's decision to discard some of Andy and John Taylor's rhythm tracks, necessitating that they be re-recorded, exposed a rift in the band that only widened in the years ahead.

'The Reflex' (Duran Duran)
Released as a single in April 1984. Chart places: UK: 1, US: 1
The up-tempo song with good bones that opens the album is quite different from the one that most casual listeners know. The remixed song was taken

into the stratosphere by Nile Rodgers, marking the beginning of a decades-long friendship and working relationship between the band and the founder of the funk act Chic.

Members of Duran Duran met Rodgers while on tour with Blondie but didn't seek out the production expertise of their musical hero until they heard 'Original Sin' by INXS, which was also produced by Rodgers, while attending a party in Melbourne, Australia, following the release of *Seven And The Ragged Tiger*. The band even brought in Jason Corsaro, who engineered on the INXS track, for the remix of 'The Reflex', which featured Michelle Cobbs (also of Chic) and B. J. Nelson, who provided the famous 'da-na-na-na' backup vocals.

Although the dancefloor-friendly remix seemed like an obvious smash hit, Capitol Records executives voiced concerns about Rodgers' reimagined version, calling it 'too Black'. But as Duran Duran were one of the biggest bands in the world at the time, the remix was ultimately released and topped the charts in both the US and the UK.

The ambiguous lyrics could be about fame or, according to Le Bon, a sexual act. However, sticking with the theme that the 'ragged tiger' in the album title means 'success', let's say the song is at least partially about the band's struggles during that time. A lyric such as 'I'm on a ride and I want to get off. But they won't slow down the roundabout', seemingly points to the wild ride the band members were on. The possible double entendre of 'So why don't you use it? Try not to bruise it' only makes the lyrics delightfully cryptic.

Musically, the synths rule the show. Rhodes' Jupiter-8 produces an off-key steel drum effect in the bridge, mixed with wood-block percussion. In fact, tuning issues at the studio threatened to hamper the overall recording of the track, but everything worked out in the end. 'I have to say that I don't personally give a toss about tuning if the character and atmosphere are right', co-producer Little told *Sound On Sound* in 2004. 'The thing about Duran Duran is that they knew what they were doing, and they were all fantastic individuals and fantastic characters. The band were driven by that quirkiness.'

'The Reflex' shows the band moving away from their new wave sound and in a funkier direction. Instead of an arty video filmed on location, the clip for 'The Reflex' spotlights the energy of the band's live stage show during their massive *Sing Blue Silver* tour. The Mulcahy-directed video includes a computer-generated image of a waterfall that now looks a bit dated but nonetheless captures a moment in time quite accurately.

'New Moon On Monday' (Duran Duran)

Released as a single in January 1984. Chart places: UK: 9, US: 10

The album's second single barely cracked the top ten in the UK and the US, but it's true to the band's art pop roots. On the synth-forward track, Le Bon delivers a Bowie-esque vocal performance that's capped by an anthemic chorus.

The video is a mini-movie filmed in France and directed by Brian Grant, a colleague of Mulcahy's, as he wasn't available. Duran Duran play members of a French resistance movement and dance in celebration at the clip's conclusion. 'New Moon On Monday' was among the first of their videos – which were always stylish – to place style over substance, with its scattershot plot and on-location shoot that didn't have the same bang for the buck as Mulcahy's videos for *Rio*.

While Andy Taylor and others have noted over the years that his guitars were often less prominent on this album than on the band's earlier work, here, they pleasantly build into the chorus. The LP marked a point in the band's music in which guitars with effects and synths combined to produce what Rhodes called a 'wall of sound'. Rhodes used his trusty Jupiter-8 and then-cutting-edge Fairlight CMI to achieve the track's layered synth sounds and made recordings of himself ripping up newspapers to produce the pops of 'fireworks', which lend an added air of celebration to the uplifting track.

'(I'm Looking For) Cracks In The Pavement' (Duran Duran)
Synths are again clearly front and centre on this track, which has a catchy melody but bears some of Le Bon's most bizarre lines, including 'Don't want to be in public. My head is full of chopstick' and 'If I had a car I'd drive it insane'. Le Bon's cryptic lyrics usually work, but they sometimes fall flat. Set at a party as it's about to begin, Le Bon sheds his skin, like the reptiles referenced on the album's lead single and on 'New Moon On Monday' ('lizard mixture'). Perhaps the odd lyrics are meant to express his confusion during a time when Duran Duran were receiving as much criticism as they were praise.

Musically, the song is a bit simplistic compared to the rest of the album, as John Taylor had gone to playing fewer notes in his basslines and Roger Taylor was pursuing a more natural drum sound, though Andy Taylor manages to add some understated guitar riffs and even a brief solo. But the synths ultimately take over, and in so doing, Duran Duran lose some of the sound that, up until then, had been their signature.

'I Take The Dice' (Duran Duran)
This song also features lyrics both odd ('Hold tight onto Daddy's bracelets') and delightful ('Catch me with your fizzy smile'). Overall, Le Bon's words seem to be another commentary on fame: 'Headline in tomorrow's papers', he sings. 'Kill that light it's so bright and you're shining it right in my eyes.' Although the melody is pleasant and the chorus is catchy, the song, with its off-kilter synth effects and percussion, is one of the album's lesser tracks. The bassline is a bit rote (for Duran Duran, at least), and the guitar is barely discernible at times.

'Of Crime And Passion' (Duran Duran)
The album gets back on track with 'Of Crime And Passion', on which Andy Taylor finally gets a chance to deliver the album's first proper guitar solo. The song, which features dramatic lyrics, is reminiscent of the band's earlier work,

such as 'Careless Memories', in which Le Bon repeatedly shouts, 'Look out!' 'Liar!' Le Bon wails this time. 'Couldn't cut me deeper with a knife if you tried'. Later, he addresses a 'bride of wire' who's also presumably the 'liar' referenced earlier. 'Saw your heart turn spade', he sings. 'This orchid's turned to black'. Both songs appear to address the break-up of a relationship, though the sense of betrayal is heightened here.

Rhodes and Taylor's playing again combines to great success. The two produce a wall of sound in the pre-chorus that Rhodes believes was played on the Fairlight and Jupiter-8 synths, as well as guitar with effects. As he told 'Ask Katy' on DuranDuran.com in 2018, 'With many Duran Duran songs, we try to combine the sound of different instruments playing together to blur the edges so that it becomes unclear precisely what is happening musically.'

'Union Of The Snake' (Duran Duran)

Released as a single in October 1983. Chart places: UK: 3, US: 3

This slinky track features funky rhythm guitar from Taylor, a sax solo from frequent contributor Andy Hamilton and sensual vocals from Le Bon. The song is another nod to Bowie, with a bass drum pattern reminiscent of 'Let's Dance'.

In the video, directed by Simon Milne and featuring the young actor and future Academy Award winner Jennifer Connelly, Le Bon plays a *Mad Max*-style warrior in an apocalyptic desert setting, and members of the band consult a map inside a cave amid writhing dancers. Although the plot is a bit confusing, the mood of the clip fits the mysterious nature of the track.

The song originated with Rhodes' experimentation on his new Fairlight synth, which he used to create layers of sound for the unique intro and middle eight section. The sounds were as distinctive as their maker, who was often seen performing live with the Fairlight using an optical pen on a monitor screen. Rhodes, who over the years has gained the nickname 'The Controller', has been characterised by some as merely being a button-pusher onstage, but his genius in the studio can't be denied. Rhodes himself has played into this narrative, alternately saying that he was 'changing sounds' and 'fiddling with wave forms' while using the light pen or just 'doing my shopping list'.

'Shadows On Your Side' (Duran Duran)

This sublime song is another highlight on the album, as it allows both Rhodes and Andy Taylor to have their moments in classic Duran Duran style, and John Taylor is ever-agile on bass. Le Bon harmonises with himself on the track, which concludes with a harmonica effect mixed with eerie synths as he repeatedly sings, 'Shadows are on your side'. The song seems to be yet another commentary on the trappings of fame, with lyrics like 'With everybody to say that you're having the time of your life when your life is on the slide'. As on their previous albums, *Seven And The Ragged Tiger* gave the band a chance to explore deeper and often darker realms, this time throughout the LP instead of solely on the B-side.

Notably, the band had never played this song live until 2011 due to the difficulty of the bassline.

'Tiger Tiger' (Duran Duran)
One of Duran Duran's most enchanting songs is also one of their few solely instrumental tracks. It prominently features John Taylor's fretless bass grooves, Rhodes' calliope-like synth melody and Hamilton's saxophone. For viewers of the documentary *Sing Blue Silver*, it's forever etched into memory as a depiction of the relentless grind of life on the road. It leads seamlessly into the album's epic closing track, and together, they make a brilliant artistic statement.

'The Seventh Stranger' (Duran Duran)
Together with 'Tiger Tiger', 'The Seventh Stranger' marks the high point of the album. Duran Duran were fast becoming known for their superb album closers, and this track is one of their best. Percussive effects open the song, on which synths and guitars meld delectably, and Taylor again shines on fretless bass. The track, which stemmed from the demo 'Seven And The Ragged Tiger', also takes inspiration from Akira Kurosawa's *Seven Samurai* films. Le Bon delivers wistful lyrics that seem to be about the non-stop carousel of fame and the endless cycle of touring: 'Can't tell the real from reflections, when all these faces look the same to me' and 'A year of Sundays seems to have drifted right by. (I could have sworn) in one evening'. The band's near-constant schedule of recording, touring and other commitments was weighing on the members, and the strain was about to become greater as they embarked on the *Sing Blue Silver* tour, their most extensive yet.

Extra Tracks

'Secret Oktober' (Duran Duran)
Like 'The Chauffeur', 'Secret Oktober' was largely Rhodes and Le Bon's creation. The two wrote the song and, along with Sadkin, completed the recording and mixing, all within 24 hours to provide the B-side of 'Union Of The Snake'. It has become a fan favourite and was re-recorded by the classic lineup, retitled 'Secret Oktober 31st', for *Danse Macabre*.

The mystical, poetic lyrics – including lines like 'Smile when the butterfly escapes the killing jar' – and music box-like synths combine to form what's arguably the band's best B-side. It's no wonder that the rest of the members wanted to add their stamp with their recent reimagining. Le Bon has declared the original track his favourite Duran Duran song.

'Make Me Smile (Come Up And See Me)' (Steve Harley)
This live version of Steve Harley & Cockney Rebel's UK number-one hit and the B-side of 'The Reflex' is a fan-favourite cover on which Duran Duran pay tribute to the glam rockers. This version starts quietly with only vocals and

keyboards (the screaming of the crowd can be heard above the music at times, as was customary at the band's live shows back then) before the rest of the instruments kick in. The track is led by Andy Taylor's blazing guitar, including a solo that seems right up his alley.

With *Seven And The Ragged Tiger*, the band caught the proverbial tiger by the tale. What came next was a period of further domination of the music world and a fracturing of the classic lineup that would take well over a decade to heal.

Other Early Singles

By 1984, Duran Duran had hit their stride after releasing a string of three smash-hit albums. They had reached a career peak with 'The Reflex' – their first single to top the charts in both the UK and the US – following their first UK number-one single the year prior.

However, three of the band's biggest hits were never originally on studio albums: 'Is There Something I Should Know?' was a stand-alone track added to a re-release of their first album in the US, 'The Wild Boys' was part of the live album *Arena* and 'A View To A Kill' was from the soundtrack of the James Bond film of the same name – each one a resounding triumph.

Around 1985, Duran Duran were never more in demand. They were followed on the *Sing Blue Silver* tour by Mulcahy, who shot footage for the successful documentary of the same name and the concert film *Arena*. On the back of 'The Wild Boys', the *Arena* album was a top-ten hit in the UK and the US, despite its shortcomings as a live record. The band won their first and only Grammy Awards – best short-form music video for 'Girls On Film'/'Hungry Like The Wolf' and best video album for *Duran Duran*. Due to touring commitments, the band weren't present at the ceremony to pick up their statuettes, a move the members have said they regret.

Duran Duran were at the height of their powers; their rise drew comparisons at the time to Beatlemania. During a press conference in Hollywood, California, attended by well over 100 journalists, the media directed questions towards each member. The proceedings took a randy turn after they were asked when they had started playing their instruments, with Le Bon famously chiming in for their drummer, 'Roger needs two hands for his!'

Also in 1984, Rhodes joined Andy and Roger Taylor in the ranks of married men when he wed Julie Anne Friedman, a model and heiress to the Younkers department store chain, at a lavish ceremony while dressed mostly in pink – and with a flock of flamingos on hand. The band members capped the year by participating in the recording of the star-studded Band Aid charity single 'Do They Know It's Christmas?', which became the 1984 Christmas number-one in the UK.

After an opportunity of a lifetime had presented itself that year, Duran Duran were selected to record the theme song to the Bond film *A View To A Kill*. John Taylor had famously approached Bond producer Albert 'Cubby' Broccoli at a party and suggested that the band perform the franchise's next theme song. Soon, Duran Duran were introduced to the legendary composer John Barry. They became the first rock band to write a Bond theme with Barry and made history as the only musical act to have a Bond song top the *Billboard* Hot 100 in the US.

'Is There Something I Should Know?' (Single, 1983)
Personnel: Simon Le Bon, Nick Rhodes, Andy Taylor, John Taylor, Roger Taylor
Recorded in December 1982 at Good Earth Studios

Producers: Duran Duran and Ian Little
Record label: EMI/Capitol
Original release date: March 1983 (UK) and May 1983 (US)
Highest chart places: UK: 1, US: 4

'Is There Something I Should Know?' (Duran Duran)

Duran Duran's first UK number-one came far easier than a nuclear war. The Beatles-esque song with that famous line ('Don't say you're easy on me. 'Cause you're about as easy as a nuclear war') was a natural hit in the band's home country.

A jangly guitar riff and pulsating Jupiter-8 synth line accompany Le Bon's plea of 'Please, please tell me now'. The abstract, stylish video, directed by Mulcahy, features the band members dressed in blue shirts with white ties tucked into them as a boy chases a red ball and a baby is mesmerised by snippets of the band's previous videos. The popular clip, which showed the members singing to the camera and not playing instruments – even though Le Bon and Andy Taylor are the only vocalists credited on the track – may have helped pigeonhole Duran Duran as a 'boy band' to some misinformed viewers. However, the members did indeed play their own instruments, and Le Bon even contributed a harmonica solo on the track.

The song was mixed by Bob Clearmountain, who had worked with Bowie, Roxy Music and others, before the band settled on a different mix by Alex Sadkin, who also worked with them on *Seven And The Ragged Tiger*.

'Faith In This Colour' (Duran Duran)

The B-side of the single is an instrumental track that may be most notable for featuring unauthorised samples taken from *Star Wars* on some pressings. This synth-heavy effort seems as if it's not fully formed as a song, especially when compared to their other early instrumentals, such as 'Tel Aviv' and 'Tiger Tiger'. Still, it's far from an unpleasant listen.

'The Wild Boys' (Single, 1984)

Personnel: Simon Le Bon, Nick Rhodes, Andy Taylor, John Taylor, Roger Taylor
Recorded in July 1984 at Maison Rouge
Producer: Nile Rodgers
Record label: EMI/Capitol
Original release date: October 1984
Highest chart places: UK: 2, US: 2

'The Wild Boys' (Duran Duran)

The band's second collaboration with Rodgers was nearly as successful as the first. The song, which features the chant 'Wild boys! Wild boys! Wild boys!', as well as keyboard stabs and hard-hitting percussion, was a number two smash on both sides of the pond. It was kept out of the top spot in the US by Daryl

Hall & John Oates' 'Out Of Touch' and Madonna's 'Like A Virgin'; in the UK, by Chaka Khan's 'I Feel For You'.

The song is said to have been inspired musically by Frankie Goes to Hollywood's hit song 'Relax' and based on *The Wild Boys: A Book Of The Dead* by William S. Burroughs. In fact, the band wrote the song at the urging of Mulcahy, who sought to direct a feature film version of Burroughs' book. While the film (and a Duran Duran soundtrack) never came to fruition, the song and video certainly made their own impact.

The budget for Mulcahy's video reportedly topped a whopping 1 million pounds, rivalling some feature films of the day. It showcases the band members dressed in *Mad Max*-style get-ups and stuck in various precarious states. John Taylor is strapped to the roof of a car and tortuously confronted with images from his past on a video screen above. Le Bon is famously bound to a windmill's blade and repeatedly submerged in a pool of water below. The choreographer for the video, Arlene Mills, claimed that the singer briefly flirted with real-life danger when the windmill stopped operating while he was underwater. She told the *Birmingham Mail Sunday Mercury* in 2021 that it turned out to be 'an amazing video, though. 'Wild Boys' was just the most fabulous, mad video ever.'

The 12" single was accompanied by a live version of '(I'm Looking For) Cracks In The Pavement' and an extended mix called 'The Wild Boys (Wilder Than The Wild Boys)'.

'A View To A Kill' (Single, 1985)
Personnel: Simon Le Bon, Nick Rhodes, Andy Taylor, John Taylor, Roger Taylor
Recorded in April 1985 at Maison Rouge
Producers: Bernard Edwards, Jason Corsaro and Duran Duran
Record label: EMI/Capitol
Original release date: May 1985
Highest chart places: UK: 2, US: 1

'A View To A Kill' (Duran Duran, John Barry)
Barry had been the primary writer of most James Bond theme songs up to 'A View To A Kill'. (Wings' 'Live And Let Die', written by Paul and Linda McCartney, was a notable exception.) But with Duran Duran, he was more of a 'sixth member' who helped weed out the band's bad ideas from the good, according to Le Bon. As co-producers, the band brought in Chic bassist Bernard Edwards, as Rodgers had a prior commitment, as well as previous collaborator Corsaro. The single included Barry's orchestral instrumental 'A View To A Kill (That Fatal Kiss)' as its B-side. Notably, a 12" remix of the single finally surfaced in 2014 but has never officially been released.

However, recording the song was far from stress-free. Roger Taylor told DuranDuran.com in 2015 that 'there was quite a lot of tension around the sessions, with pressure to deliver a hit in a week's time', and in front of John

Taylor's bass hero, no less. While the rhythm section laid down their parts for the track relatively quickly, tensions arose between Rhodes and Barry. According to John and Andy Taylor in their respective memoirs, Rhodes butted heads with the composer, and disagreements arose over musical matters.

Nevertheless, the collaborators managed to deliver the song and scored a timeless hit. The music fitted seamlessly into the Bond style, yet was performed in a fresh, new way by one of the biggest bands in the world at the time. Rhodes' keyboard stabs, Andy Taylor's funky guitar riffs and Le Bon's lyrics, including those in the epic chorus – 'Dance into the fire. That fatal kiss is all you need' – cemented the track as one of the highlights to come out of actor Roger Moore's final Bond film.

For the video, the band again employed Godley & Creme ('Girls On Film') for an action-packed shoot at the Eiffel Tower, footage from which was woven together with scenes from the film. Andy Taylor plays a blind musician, almost gleefully disabling Rhodes (in the role of a photographer) via his earpiece by pressing a key on his accordion. The clip ends with Le Bon delivering his now-famous line: 'Bon, Simon Le Bon'.

The scene between Rhodes and Taylor, though all in good fun, proved somewhat prophetic. Taylor, after side projects had planted the seeds for his next endeavour, reportedly made the decision to leave the band on the day of the video shoot. 'A View To A Kill' stood as the last studio recording by the Fab Five for nearly two decades.

Notorious (1986)

Personnel:
Simon Le Bon: vocals
Nick Rhodes: keyboards
John Taylor: bass
Steve Ferrone: drums
Andy Taylor: guitars
Nile Rodgers: guitars
Additional musicians:
Warren Cuccurullo: guitars
Max Gollehon: horns
Jimmy Maelen: percussion
The Borneo Horns (Lenny Pickett, Steve Elson, Stan Harrison): horns
Curtis King Jr.: vocals
Brenda White-King: vocals
Tessa Niles: vocals
Cindy Mizelle: vocals
Recorded at Studio Davout, Abbey Road Studios, Westside Studios, Maison Rouge, Skyline and AIR Studios' from June to September 1986
Produced by Nile Rodgers with Duran Duran
Engineer: Daniel Abraham
Record label: EMI/Capitol
Release date: November 1986
Highest chart places: UK: 16, US: 12
Running time: 46:56
Current edition: 2024 Warner Music CD/LP

Leading up to the release of the smash James Bond theme song 'A View To A Kill', Duran Duran splintered into separate groups. Andy Taylor, keen to play more straight-ahead rock music, formed The Power Station, a supergroup with John Taylor, Chic drummer Tony Thompson, blue-eyed soul singer Robert Palmer and Chic's Bernard Edwards as producer. Le Bon and Rhodes went in a more esoteric direction with Arcadia, which was aided by a variety of famous musical guests and producer Alex Sadkin. Roger Taylor, ever the peace-oriented 'quiet one', diplomatically contributed to The Power Station's album despite being a member of Arcadia.

The Power Station was hugely successful, especially in the US, where their self-titled album, released in March 1985, and lead single 'Some Like It Hot' both hit number six on the *Billboard* charts. Their second single, a cover of T. Rex's 'Get It On', also cracked the US top ten, at number nine. They played *Saturday Night Live* and even had a cameo appearance on *Miami Vice* on US television. But any long-term hopes that the band would continue fizzled when Palmer passed on touring with them as his solo career took off.

Arcadia's ethereal, synth-driven *So Red The Rose*, released in November 1985, featured a range of guest artists, including Grace Jones, Sting, David Gilmour of Pink Floyd, Carlos Alomar, Herbie Hancock and Andy Mackay of Roxy Music. The 'Election Day' single charted in the top ten in the UK and the US, and the album achieved platinum sales status. In addition to working with Duran Duran producer Sadkin, Arcadia worked with Mulcahy on the video for 'The Flame', which also featured a cameo appearance by John Taylor.

The two factions came together on 13 July 1985 to headline Live Aid, a massive worldwide charity concert organised by Bob Geldof. However, at the Philadelphia show, it didn't look as if the band members were even part of the same group. Andy and John Taylor were in full-on rocker mode. (They also played with The Power Station, featuring touring singer Michael Des Barres.) Le Bon, Rhodes and Roger Taylor had embraced a goth image with their hair dyed black. It didn't seem as if there was a clear path forward for a band that had been an unstoppable unit for more than five years.

Still, Le Bon and Rhodes wanted Duran Duran to continue, though whether all the Taylors would join them was uncertain. John Taylor was easily sold on regrouping, according to his memoir, *In The Pleasure Groove: Love, Death & Duran Duran*, and he then attempted to get Roger and Andy on board. But Roger Taylor had gotten a taste of the quiet life away from the glare of celebrity and declined. Andy Taylor's status was still unclear, though he wrote in his own memoir, *Wild Boy*, that he'd already made his decision to leave the band by then.

It was clear that the members' relationship with the Berrows had run its course. John and Andy Taylor believed that the managers were no longer working in the interests of the band. Rhodes grew to share that view, especially in the wake of Le Bon's near-drowning on Drum, a yacht co-owned by the singer and the Berrows. Though Le Bon enjoyed yachting (and even recorded the song 'Grey Lady Of The Sea' for the documentary *Drum: A Journey Of A Lifetime*), he had taken significant time away from the band to participate in the Fastnet Race in 1985. After Drum capsized and Le Bon and the rest of the crew were rescued, his brush with death apparently was the final straw, and the band parted ways with their long-time managers.

With three members on board, Duran Duran waded into uncertain waters with their fourth studio album, *Notorious*. They again joined forces with Rodgers, who was a steady hand as a producer and a masterful guitar player who could fill in as they waited for Andy Taylor to arrive. Some clarity surrounding Taylor's status came when the studio received an unsolicited phone call from another guitarist: Warren Cuccurullo, an accomplished player known for his work with Frank Zappa and Missing Persons. He was a brash Brooklynite who, like Missing Persons' vocalist Dale Bozzio, had posed nude in an American magazine. Cuccurullo seemed determined to shape his future with the English group. After all, his band had split up, and drummer Terry Bozzio and bassist Patrick O'Hearn were now working with Andy Taylor, of all people, in Los Angeles. After Cuccurullo shared this news with Duran Duran, he joined the band in the studio as a session guitarist.

Taylor, who had sung lead with Palmer on The Power Station's cover of The Isley Brothers' 'Harvest For The World', signed a solo recording contract with major label MCA Records and went on to release two albums, *Thunder* and *Dangerous*. Meanwhile, Duran Duran, with Cuccurullo on board, abandoned efforts to get Taylor back into the studio.

The band, now a three-piece, employed more studio musicians than ever before, including a horn section. Also new to the fold was drummer Steve Ferrone of The Average White Band, an accomplished session player. With Rodgers at the helm, it only made sense that the music headed in a funkier direction. Rodgers, one of the band's biggest champions, nudged them to continually progress as musicians, pushing them to eventually become a widely respected act. He told *Spinner* in 2011:

> I used to say to the guys, 'People don't realise how great you are because you're still like this boy band, and the girls are still talking about your looks. The music becomes sort of an added bonus. Now, it's time to go in a direction where you can become more like a U2 that's really classic and solid artistically. You gotta build that foundation, and let's take the fans along with us.'

While their music was beefed up with an array of hired hands, the trio's streamlined image may have been jarring to young fans of a band that had been marketed as teen idols and had even been the subject of a Milton Bradley board game geared for players aged seven and over. The *Notorious* album served as a reminder that Andy and Roger Taylor were no longer in the picture. Its cover features a black-and-white image by photographer John Swannell of the three remaining band members suavely dressed in black suits. On the back is a photo of model Christy Turlington, with the overall design by Frank Olinsky of Manhattan Design.

Notorious was the first real test for a band that had tasted success right out of the gate. Le Bon, Rhodes and Taylor daringly charted a new course without the managers who had helped steer the ship since the start. Their fourth album signalled their willingness to experiment as they embraced a more mature sound and image – they had faith that their fans would follow.

'Notorious' (Duran Duran)

Released as a single in October 1986. Chart places: UK: 7, US: 2

'Notorious' was the upbeat single that the band needed in 1986. Featuring funky guitar riffs by Rodgers, equally funky bass by Taylor, liberal use of horns and synths closer to resembling traditional keyboards than perhaps any that Rhodes had played before, the song was a hit in both the UK and the US. Rhodes had moved towards using mostly digital synths at the time, resulting in the icy-cool sound on much of *Notorious*.

Lyrically, the song is a statement of defiance by a band many had written off. 'Fools run rings to break up. Something they'll never destroy', Le Bon sings. The track also includes a reference to 'a flaky bandit' – widely believed to mean Andy Taylor.

In addition to being a success upon its release, the track has held up, aided by high-profile references in pop culture. Years after it stormed the charts, it was resurrected by rapper The Notorious B.I.G. and used in the cult film *Donnie Darko* during a scene in which the 'Sparkle Motion' dance group performs.

The black-and-white video, directed by Peter Kagan and Paula Greif, features a performance by the band with Rodgers, Turlington and dancers choreographed by future pop star Paula Abdul. The clip is strikingly similar to Steve Winwood's video for 'Higher Love', which was directed by Kagan and Greif and featured Rodgers, who also played rhythm guitar on the Winwood track.

When the band played their new songs live, the members said that for the first time in years, they could hear themselves playing instead of the audience screaming. With a slick new image and a funkier sound, there was no doubt that this wasn't a boy band. This was Duran Duran, all grown up.

'American Science' (Duran Duran)

Duran Duran further explore their more mature side on the album's second track, the sultry 'American Science'. A mere three years earlier, it would have been hard to imagine that the Duran Duran of *Seven And The Ragged Tiger* would be recording songs like this one.

Horns open the track before Rhodes' atmospheric synths kick in. The song features stunningly direct lyrics from Le Bon. 'Don't keep me waiting, come and lie beside me', he tells the subject, for whom 'there ain't a thing you can't acquire with your cling-wrap plaything' – a line that seems quite sexual.

Andy Taylor is widely credited as playing the track's first guitar solo, and the listener gets their first taste of Cuccurullo's often virtuosic playing during his EBow solo later in the song. Rodgers no doubt contributes rhythm guitar, as he does on the majority of the album, while Ferrone plays a mix of programmed and live drums on the track.

'Skin Trade' (Duran Duran)

Released as a single in January (US) and February 1987 (UK). Chart places: UK: 22, US: 39

The album's second single, with its title inspired by the book *Adventures In The Skin Trade* by Dylan Thomas, as well as its nod to blue-eyed soul and a Prince-esque falsetto, couldn't be further away from the band's previous hit songs, and its chart showing was subpar.

The trio had a sense of insecurity over the future during the promotion for *Notorious,* as evidenced in the documentary *Three To Get Ready*. Taylor didn't understand why 'Skin Trade' wasn't burning up the charts, even proclaiming that it was 'an infinitely better song than 'Wild Boys'.' It didn't help matters that bands like U2 and INXS, who, until that point, had been less successful than Duran Duran, were just now hitting their stride.

But chart performance isn't an indication of a song's quality. Le Bon's vocals are especially good as he takes his voice to new places, adopting a more refined singing style and employing falsetto here and throughout the album. Rhodes' smooth synths, Taylor's ever-funky bass, Ferrone's drumming (he used a 'gated' drum sound on much of the LP) and a trumpet solo round out the track. The song, which was a stylistic leap for the band into a more mature r&b-influenced sound, also features the line for which they named their successful tour: 'Would someone please explain. The reason for this strange behaviour'. Cuccurullo, not yet an official member of the band, plays power chords and a distorted harmony part in the bridge of the song and even appears in the video. The colourful clip, again directed by Kagan and Greif, features shots of the band members performing, as well as model Tatjana Patitz.

In addition, Duran Duran became a victim of censorship (and possibly sold fewer copies of the single) when the artwork, featuring a silhouette of a naked bum, was banned and a plain red cover was used instead.

'A Matter Of Feeling' (Duran Duran)

Lyrically and musically, this song could be a more mature version of 'Save A Prayer'. Rhodes' synths on the track hark back to that ballad, and Le Bon, instead of singing about a one-night stand, delves deeper, perhaps as a man looking back on his past. 'Steal away in the morning, love's already history to you', he sings. Later, he reflects hopefully, 'Tears will dry as you're leaving. Who knows you might find something to last'.

At a time when Duran Duran were discovering that their musical career wasn't always going to be smooth sailing, on *Notorious*, Le Bon displayed a confidence that seemed as boundless as ever. After all, he had survived a yachting accident and his band's near-implosion and was newly married to a supermodel, Yasmin Le Bon.

With three guitarists in the mix, or four, since apparently John Taylor also played rhythm guitar during the sessions, it isn't entirely clear who's playing on which tracks. But Andy Taylor is believed to have contributed the subtle riffs heard on 'A Matter Of Feeling'.

'Hold Me' (Duran Duran)

This upbeat rocker features blazing guitars from Cuccurullo and jaunty keyboards by Rhodes. The expert rhythm section of Taylor and Ferrone lay down a driving beat as Le Bon implores the subject of the song to 'Hold me. Lay your ghosts away. Show me for yourself'. His vocals soar in the chorus, punctuated by guitar riffs, and a keyboard-heavy instrumental break leads into the bridge.

The track was originally titled 'Rope' in reference to the Alfred Hitchcock film of the same name. The legendary director's work also inspired two other tracks on the album, 'Notorious' and 'Vertigo (Do The Demolition)'.

'Vertigo (Do The Demolition)' (Duran Duran)
This moody song takes its cues from the film noir for which it's named. Rhodes' atmospheric synths open the track, and Cuccurullo's distorted guitar riffs play off the keyboards throughout. The synth work on *Notorious* is understated at times, with horns – including The Borneo Horns, also heard on the Bowie album *Tonight* – often filling the space usually taken up by Rhodes' typical layers of sound. Yet, this song allows both the synths and the guitars to shine, a combination that's a hallmark of the band's earlier work.

'So Misled' (Duran Duran)
The album takes a chill turn with this track, which starts with ambient drums fading in and ends with the music and vocals fading out. In addition, it veers into Chic territory with its funky guitar and female backup vocals. Its lyrics seem to address addiction, with lines like 'Now my body's got to use it' and a repeated chorus of 'I should not be so misled'. Le Bon briefly slips into a cockney lilt as he says 'Okay, take it away' before the backup singers close out the track.

It wasn't the only time that the band would address addiction in their music. In the UK tabloids, they had already been branded as 'coke crazy Duran Duran', based on a club doorman's account of their long-ago exploits at the Rum Runner, a move that the members saw as a betrayal.

'Meet El Presidente' (Duran Duran)
Released as a single in April 1987. Chart places: UK: 24, US: 70
This song, which was remixed to appeal to Latin music fans in the US with an emphasis on percussion and horns, stalled on the charts and remains a questionable choice for a third single. Duranies saw a missed opportunity, as 'A Matter Of Feeling' or 'Hold Me' might have had the potential to reach a wider audience. However, the band appeared dead set on forging ahead with new sounds and breaking ground in their own career, though not necessarily on the charts. They seemed more interested in channelling *Young Americans*-era Bowie, from a performance of the song on *Soul Train* to the use of black-and-white promo footage during the period. In 1987, they joined his *Glass Spider* tour, seizing the rare chance to open for one of their musical heroes. Yet, 'Meet El Presidente' has a pleasant melody and lyrics by Le Bon, referencing politics and sex, about a 'Miss November Tuesday' who 'you've never refused when she lies back. Put a stripe on the union, a star on the jack'.

Kagan and Greif once again helmed the video, which captured the band's performance as seen on their *Strange Behaviour* tour.

'Winter Marches On' (Duran Duran)
This sublime song is a highlight of the album. The slow-burning track opens with bells and Arcadia-esque synths. The bass, played on a Synclavier synth, resembles the sound of an upright bass.

With the chorus – 'Loud is the music the crowd is bringing. Out of my head as the winter marches on' – this quietly beautiful song was a departure for the band on an album of mostly upbeat, funky tracks. Le Bon's standout vocals and an angelic chorus of backup singers helped to make the track unlike anything the band had recorded before. With the addition of more traditional sounds, such as upright bass, to the band's synth repertoire, as well as the ballad's solemn lyrics, the song could be seen as a sophisticated spin on their artier classics, like 'The Chauffeur'.

'Proposition' (Duran Duran)
The final track on *Notorious* is part of a pantheon of epic album closers by the band. Horns blare full force, driving the track, along with Taylor's thumping bassline.

Le Bon's socially conscious lyrics seem to be about a desperate woman and a child who 'pay for the crime of feeling'. "Bring back that child', she said', he sings, suggesting that the woman and child have become separated, likely through no fault of their own. 'When all your pride is dead', he sings about her predicament, 'You must be scared instead'.

In addition to Le Bon's soaring vocals, the track features some funky rhythm guitar, likely by Rodgers or performed in his style, as well as an exhilarating instrumental break dominated by keyboards, bass and heavier riffs.

Extra Tracks

'We Need You' (Duran Duran)
The B-side to 'Skin Trade' is the only song from the *Notorious* era to feature only the three band members. The track, which is similar to The Rolling Stones' 'We Love You', was recorded during a late-night session. John Taylor, who came up with the simple guitar part, told 'Ask Katy' on DuranDuran.com in 2003 that it was 'perhaps the purest song of that season.'

Indeed, the stripped-down, lyrically tender track is arguably one of their finest B-sides. Musically, the song is striking in its simplicity, as Rhodes plays a basic keyboard line in addition to lush yet subtle synths. The lyrics are more complex. Le Bon sings wistfully, 'You look sharp inside your pointed shoes. I have this picture hanging in my room', which could be about an old flame or even a former bandmate.

In the extended outro to the song, Le Bon harmonises with himself as he repeatedly sings, 'We need you'. Though the song's subject has been rumoured to be Andy Taylor, the band never confirmed this. In fact, they've acknowledged the track's similarities to The Stones' song, which in turn has been interpreted as a thank-you to that band's fans. So, 'you' and 'we' likely

mean the fans and Duran Duran, who, in the wake of their first album as a trio, needed them more than ever.

Big Thing (1988)

Personnel:
Simon Le Bon: vocals
Nick Rhodes: keyboards, vocals
John Taylor: bass, vocals
Warren Cuccurullo: guitars
Steve Ferrone: drums
Additional musicians:
Jonathan Elias: keyboards, vocals
Chester Kamen: guitars
Daniel Abraham: guitar on 'Do You Believe In Shame?'
Marc Chantereau: percussion
Louis Cesar Ewande: urban jungle drums
Stan Harrison: saxophone
Patrick Bourgoin: saxophone
David Tofani: saxophone
Max Gollehon: trumpet
Glenn Ferris: trombone
Joniece Jamison: vocals on 'Big Thing' and 'I Don't Want Your Love'
Carole Fredericks: vocals on 'Big Thing', 'I Don't Want Your Love', 'Too Late Marlene', 'Land'
Yvonne Jones: vocals on 'Too Late Marlene' and 'Land'
Beckie Bell: vocals on 'Too Late Marlene' and 'Land'
Recorded at Studio Davout from 1987 to 1988
Produced by Duran Duran, Jonathan Elias and Daniel Abraham
Engineer: Daniel Abraham
Record label: EMI/Capitol
Release date: October 1988
Highest chart places: UK: 15, US: 24
Running time: 44:48
Current edition: 2024 Warner Music CD/LP

Following *Notorious*, Duran Duran found themselves in a new situation. They had experienced their first commercial disappointment when two of the three singles on the previous album failed to break through on the charts in both the UK and the US. So, it was time once again to tweak the band's DNA.

They decided to explore house music and experimental sounds and brought on a new producer, Jonathan Elias, whom they had met while recording 'A View To A Kill'. Previously, Elias had worked on solo material with John Taylor, including the minor hit 'I Do What I Do' from the film *9½ Weeks*. Daniel Abraham, the engineer on *Notorious*, was again enlisted as the engineer as well as an additional producer. Elias had a keen interest in Indigenous and world music, and instruments, including 'urban jungle drums', were added to the mix on songs like 'Lake Shore Driving'. Members of the band also worked with Elias on his own project, released in 1989, *Requiem For The Americas: Songs From The Lost World*, which featured the track 'Follow In My Footsteps', written and sung by Le Bon with Susanna Hoffs of The Bangles.

Duran Duran were still officially a threesome but had a key player adding a new dimension to their sound. Cuccurullo, who had joined the recording sessions for *Notorious* later in the process, brought guitars to the forefront on *Big Thing*. Cuccurullo, who had also played on the extensive *Strange Behaviour* tour, was among a lengthy list of musicians to join the band in the studio. They included drummer Steve Ferrone, as well as guitarist Chester Kamen, who had worked with Paul McCartney and Bryan Ferry.

The band's image was equally in flux. Le Bon grew out his hair, like fellow lead singer Michael Hutchence of INXS, who became a close friend in the years ahead. Rhodes was still platinum blonde, and Taylor was rail thin. For the first time since *Rio*, there was no photo of the band members on the album cover, only artwork by Swiss illustrator and graphic designer Hans Arnold. During this period, they stylised their name as Duranduran, almost as if to distance themselves from their past. In a similar marketing move, the band's new manager, Peter Rudge (who had also worked with The Rolling Stones), asked Capitol Records to send the guitar-heavy single 'LSD Edit' to radio stations under The Krush Brothers name instead of Duran Duran.

Musically, the studio team sought a new direction but engaged in a tug-of-war over just what that path would be, according to the band members. Abraham, who leaned more toward the rock side of things, worked during the day, then Rhodes, with Elias, arrived in the evening and made changes to the material. 'It was an interesting time for us, actually, as a band', Rhodes said in the 2018 audio retrospective *Big Thing 30*. 'We were looking for a new direction, which is nothing new because we're always looking for a new direction.'

Though the band members were at odds at times, they managed to meet in the middle on songs such as 'All She Wants Is'. The cutting-edge electronic track is part of the A-side of the album, which is mostly a dance record, while the B-side is reserved for rock ballads, instrumental snippets and guitar experimentation. Despite all the push and pull over the album's musical direction, the final product is remarkably cohesive.

'Big Thing' (Duran Duran)

The album starts on an off note with the lyrically questionable title track. The chorus, sung by the 'Big Voice Chorus', consisting of Taylor, Rhodes and a host of others, includes lines like 'Bang it up, bang it out, banging on a big thing'. The band members have stated that lyrics like 'Get it out, get it in time' are meant as a tongue-in-cheek view of the marketing of albums in the recording industry – apparently a sexually suggestive double entendre. The lyrics were the result of 'a tragic group effort', according to Taylor. 'It is one of the worst lyrics we have ever written, so bad in fact, that perhaps it justifies all the criticism that has ever been levelled at us!' the bassist told 'Ask Katy' on DuranDuran.com in 2011.

The song is on more solid ground musically. Abraham references the snare drum sound created by producer Trevor Horn for Yes on *Big Generator*. Cuccurullo's guitar work is a highlight of the track, which also prominently features a horn section. Taylor plays synth bass, as he does on much of the album's A-side.

'I Don't Want Your Love' (Duran Duran)
Released as a single in September 1988. Chart places: UK: 14, US: 4
The album's second track is driven by dynamic bass and percussion, horns, 'noise' guitar from Kamen and rhythm guitar by both Cuccurullo and Kamen. The single, a remix by Shep Pettibone, was a big hit, especially in Italy, where it was the year's top-selling single, and the US.

The chorus is perfect for singing along to, and in the bridge, Le Bon provides some contrast by speaking the line 'I like noise 'cause I like waking up the house. I cannot sit down. I can't shut my mouth' before launching back into a higher register.

The video, directed by Steve Lowe, features a big-haired Cuccurullo miming Kamen's solo, as well as David Palmer, formerly of ABC, on drums. (Ferrone played on the album track.) The clip, set in a courtroom, features Le Bon, Rhodes and Taylor as they testify before a judge and tabloid reporters. People in the courtroom hold publications with screaming headlines such as 'Duran Duran Exposé: Courtroom Shock'. But the band members appear assured of their innocence, each one mouthing the lyrics in one of their videos once again, perhaps now confident that their string of more mature songs had proved that they were no longer a 'boy band'.

'All She Wants Is' (Duran Duran)
Released as a single in December 1988. Chart places: UK: 9, US: 22
On the album's first two tracks, Rhodes takes a bit of a back seat, but its third song and second single is synth-heavy. It features a chanted chorus by Le Bon, 'lead vamp guitar' by Cuccurullo and additional guitar by Kamen.

Even though this track features the band experimenting with modern synth sounds and thumping bass more oriented towards the dance floor, it was still a chart success, especially in the UK. The sexually suggestive lyrics, sounds of female pleasure and Le Bon's yelps are further stabs at maturity. Although the repeated title dominates the lyrics, the song also includes witty lines like 'Spend your money on the corner now. You know you've gotta save some for the shoeshine boy' and 'Divine intervention couldn't keep the word from leaking out' that appear to be about a person's tawdry behaviour – perhaps involving prostitutes – that they want to cover up.

The video, directed by Dean Chamberlain, won an MTV Video Music Award for innovation. Chamberlain, a photographer, filmed the clip in the style of still photography, a time-consuming process that led Rhodes to suggest that it feature dummies of the band members' likenesses, reportedly to spare them from having to be present for much of the shoot.

'Too Late Marlene' (Duran Duran)
This jazzy song provides a break in the album's dance-driven first half with its more traditional keyboards, including a piano-synth loop, as well as a sax solo by David Tofani. Le Bon sings about the object of his affection: 'I've seen you every night, been making out since then. And still I wonder why everybody's saying that ice is thin'. The vocal harmonies are especially good on this track, as he's joined by a trio of backup singers. The song is a sultry, melancholic and mature statement that's well-placed on the album between songs about sex and drugs.

'Drug (It's Just A State of Mind)' (Duran Duran)
After this up-tempo dance track was earmarked as a potential single, remixes of the song were made. When one of the remixed versions was selected for the original tracklist of the album, it became such a contentious matter that it reportedly prompted Taylor to nearly quit the band. Duran Duran intended the song to be a 'wide-screen' production with horns, backup vocals and percussion. However, the remix merely 'presented the track in the dance style of the moment', and its inclusion was 'a big mistake' as it 'compromised the integrity and sonic flow of this particular album', Taylor said on a card included in the 2010 remastered edition, on which it was finally restored to the non-remixed Daniel Abraham version. Indeed, the non-remix is a marked improvement. The song is slowed down, allowing the bass and guitar to come to the forefront. Yet, overall, the track is dragged down by its repetitive lyrics.

'Do You Believe In Shame?' (Eleanor Broadwater, Dale Hawkins, Stanley J. Lewis, Duran Duran)
Released as a single in April 1989. Chart places: UK: 30, US: 72
The album's third single is dedicated to producer Alex Sadkin, who died in a motor accident in 1987; artist Andy Warhol, a close friend of Rhodes who also succumbed that year following gallbladder surgery; and David Miles, a childhood friend of Le Bon's who suffered a fatal drug overdose in 1986. The song, the first of three written in memory of Miles, marked new territory for Le Bon's lyric writing as he began to explore grief and overcoming it.

He begins the track in a lower register before going higher for the line 'Come out' and the chorus. 'And it may seem selfish now', he sings. 'But I'll hold on to the memory until all this fear is washed away', indicating that he's working through his grief but not yet ready to let go of the memories of his late friend. Rhodes' understated keyboards and Taylor's subtle bassline, with its flourish towards the song's conclusion, are also highlights. Yet, the sombre ballad, which was featured in the 1988 film *Tequila Sunrise*, didn't fare as well on the charts as the album's first two singles.

The video, helmed by Chinese film director Chen Kaige, is one of the band's artiest clips. Each of the members plays a character with his own storyline. Rhodes, looking a bit like Warhol, appears at an auction and in an old photo with another man who's holding a snow globe. Toward the end of the clip, he throws away the snow globe and other items from the auction. Taylor, thin and almost sickly looking, is shown with a child celebrating her birthday and later crosses paths with Rhodes inside a church. Le Bon walks on a New York City street, smiling as he watches a blind man successfully navigate a crosswalk. He also rides a tram, dropping an envelope reading 'Do you believe in shame?' to the ground below. At the end of the clip, the three meet in a room as dominoes fall in the pattern of a question mark. Exactly what this all means is open to interpretation, yet the overarching theme of the video seems to match the song, which is about grief and the process of letting go.

While Le Bon's lyrics and the video were truly inspired, the song's melody sparked a legal challenge over its similarity to Dale Hawkins' 'Suzie Q' (later recorded by Creedence Clearwater Revival and The Rolling Stones). 'Do You Believe In Shame?' was subsequently credited to the writers of the Hawkins song, as well as to Duran Duran.

'Palomino' (Duran Duran)

The album veers into more experimental territory with 'Palomino'. The track features one of Le Bon's best vocal performances on the album and what's described in the liner notes as 'liquid slowhand guitar', a bluesy style of playing by Cuccurullo. Le Bon again explores the limits of his voice, starting the song in a lower register, his vocals slightly warbling as he sings, 'She surrenders her voices. They gather, on the wind'. Then, he whispers, 'Talking, chanting, breathing into her body'. The lyrics, inspired by the female subject as well as Pablo Picasso, are among Le Bon's most fascinating. 'Painting eyes, thick, with the colour she brings in', he sings. His words bring to mind a painter giving life to their subject, whether human or animal. Indeed, during Picasso's 'blue period', when the artist ran out of blue paint, he said that he would 'use red instead', a quote referenced in the lyrics.

Midway through the song, the sound of a horse can be heard as Rhodes noodles on the keys. The track is one of the more esoteric in the band's catalogue and almost seems as if it wouldn't work with its mix of slowhand guitar, keyboard noodling and cryptic lyrics, but it's actually a highlight on the album.

'Interlude One' (Duran Duran)

This brief instrumental serves as a bridge between songs, though it's questionable whether the track is necessary at all. The song, consisting of sped-up noise, and the album's 'Flute Interlude' (as well as later instrumentals, including those on *Pop Trash*) are among the band's only truly throwaway material.

'Land' (Duran Duran)
This haunting ballad again gives Le Bon and Cuccurullo a chance to shine with soaring vocals and riffs reverberating throughout. The poetic lyrics seem to tell the tale of a long-distance love affair. 'Baby, just hear my story', Le Bon sings. 'Before I leave, before we write the end'.

Taylor's understated bassline and Rhodes' atmospheric synths form a sonic landscape for Le Bon's vocals and Cuccurullo's playing on both acoustic and electric guitar. On this album, the ballads are the standout tracks, each one seemingly better than the last.

'Flute Interlude' (Duran Duran)
Like 'Interlude One', this track consists mainly of noise, including the sound of a flute. It's almost jarring, especially as it's placed between two beautiful songs, 'Land' and 'The Edge Of America'. Perhaps both 'Interludes' are meant to be palate cleansers during an otherwise appealing run of songs.

'The Edge Of America' (Duran Duran)
This ballad again sets a high bar. The powerful lyrics seem to refer to an immigrant who encounters 'vigilantes out on dawn patrol' and 'the towers of the citadel' as he walks the edge of America. Le Bon appears to be the voice of the country's leadership as he sings, 'And we say, Hey boy, give your dreams a rest ... Learn to love your anger now. Anger here is all you possess'. It was confirmed that the lyrics are a commentary on human immigration (as well as bird migration) when the band released a video for the song to mark the 30th anniversary of the album. The clip, created with artist David Medina, depicts 'a clash between nature and culture', according to Rhodes.

Atmospheric keys and Le Bon's vocals dominate the relatively brief track, which sets the stage for the brilliant album closer.

'Lake Shore Driving' (Duran Duran)
This fine instrumental, a continuation of 'The Edge Of America', is a showcase for Cuccurullo's guitar work. Both tracks were inspired by Chicago's Lake Shore Drive, the famous road near the shoreline of Lake Michigan, and the title also possibly references an illicit drug, as in 'The Krush Brothers LSD Edit' – an edited version of 'The Edge Of America' with the addition of 'Lake Shore Driving'. Following the two 'Interludes', this song redeems the band as far as their excellent track record with instrumentals goes. It's also a great album closer, its music ending abruptly to bring the song and the LP to a fitting end.

Extra Tracks

'I Believe/All I Need To Know' (Duran Duran)

One of Duran Duran's finest B-sides graces the 'All She Wants Is' single. Rhodes' chiming keyboard line, additional piano and a harmonica solo accompany a top-notch melody and cryptic lyrics from Le Bon. He explores the lower end of his range, singing, 'I was tempted by the devil in this deep blue swimming pool. Until the devil's makeup ran'. The song, which harks back to past B-sides like 'We Need You' and 'Secret Oktober' in its simpler production style, would have been a welcome addition to the album. A full, extended version was included in the 2010 remastered package.

'God (London)' (Duran Duran)

For the B-side of 'Do You Believe In Shame?', Le Bon delivers a spoken-word performance of lyrics that reference US President Ronald Reagan, the Iran-Contra affair and The Stones' 'Sympathy For The Devil'. The track is a rare political statement to bear the band's name and opened their *Big Thing Live* tour, pointing to the members' maturity and political awakening. 'Back in our innocence, we used to simply stick two fingers up and say, 'Fuck the queen", he states in the track's lyrics. 'That was about all you had to say anyway, and then go back to the more important business of making music'. Although Duran Duran have mostly stuck to just making music, this track proves that they aren't averse to making the occasional and well-timed political statement.

'This Is How A Road Gets Made' (Duran Duran)

A second, shorter track accompanied 'God (London)' on the B-side of the third single. The spoken-word track consists of Le Bon's poem about how a road gets made and references nature instead of the politics of 'God (London)'. The band used the track as a lead-in to 'Winter Marches On' during the *Big Thing Live* tour.

Liberty (1990)

Personnel:
Simon Le Bon: vocals
Nick Rhodes: keyboards
John Taylor: bass
Warren Cuccurullo: guitars
Sterling Campbell: drums
Additional musicians:
John Jones: keyboards, programming
Spike Edney: additional keyboards, engineering
Stan Harrison: saxophone
Luís Jardim: percussion
Roddy Lorimer: trumpet
Bernard Fowler: vocals
Carol Kenyon: vocals
Tessa Niles: vocals
Recorded at Olympic Studios from May 1989 to March 1990
Produced by Chris Kimsey with Duran Duran
Engineer: Christopher Marc Potter
Record label: Parlophone/Capitol
Release date: August 1990
Highest chart places: UK: 8, US: 46
Running time: 50:26
Current edition: out of print

As Duran Duran closed in on the end of the decade that had defined them, they again looked for a new direction. Although *Big Thing* yielded two singles that performed well on the charts, its sales had dropped from those of *Notorious*. So, they attempted to go back to the start, becoming a five-piece band again, adding as official members Cuccurullo and their touring drummer, Sterling Campbell, a fellow New Yorker who had previously worked with Cyndi Lauper. 'We realised that to get the best out of a drummer and a guitarist, we really had to involve them in the songwriting process', Taylor said in the electronic press kit for the new album, *Liberty*.

Also in the vein of looking back while looking forward, on the *Big Thing Live* tour, the band played some of their early hits as 'mash-ups' with their newer songs, including 'All She Wants Is'/'Planet Earth' and 'The Wild Boys'/'Drug'. In addition, the band released their first greatest hits collection, *Decade,* which featured cover art of Le Bon, Rhodes and Taylor as illustrated by artist Stephen Sprouse. Promotional efforts for the popular collection included a new single, 'Burning The Ground' – a mash-up-style remix that featured several of their past hits and charted at number 31 in the UK – which didn't even appear on *Decade*. The single was accompanied by a video featuring Cuccurullo and, especially puzzling, Campbell, though neither was an official member when the featured songs were released, and the drummer wasn't even credited as playing on any of them.

Less than two years after *Big Thing*, the band intended to harness the energy from their live shows into an album's worth of new material. They again sought a new producer and found Chris Kimsey, a self-professed admirer of the band who, like then-manager Peter Rudge, was known for his work with The Rolling Stones. As Kimsey told SuperDeluxeEdition.com in 2020:

> It was a different Duran Duran. I went down to a rehearsal and heard some songs – there were some, although it was a bit thin on the ground, but there was pressure from the record company to do an album. 'We need it now!' I don't mind dealing with that pressure; I can help people with that pressure, but I can't help people write brilliant songs if they're not there.

The result was *Liberty*, an uneven, rock-oriented album with fewer high points than the band's previous LPs, even for some of the most die-hard Duranies. The album's artwork, which was taken at La Foire du Trône in Paris and follows a funfair theme, includes a cover photo of all five members shot by photographer Ellen von Unwerth and 'Duran Duran' in bright orange lettering. The album is currently out of print.

The band decided to forgo a promotional tour after the LP's release and instead go back into the studio to amass even more new songs to play live in the years to come. In retrospect, that decision may not have been the wisest one at the time, at least as far as the fate of their newest album went.

The band hadn't yet realised that they had already found an ideal producer in John Jones, who had put together 'Burning The Ground', contributed keyboards and programming for *Liberty* and could ably steer the ship into a new decade. But history can never be rewritten, of course, and without the career low they were about to hit, their future could have been far different.

In typical Duran Duran fashion, the band had to falter first before finding their path forward.

'Violence Of Summer (Love's Taking Over)' (Duran Duran)
Released as a single in July 1990. Chart places: UK: 20, US: 64
The first single, with its awkward lyrics, sank the album's chances of success from the get-go. The song's weak chart performance – though it did hit number two in Italy – wasn't helped by the fact that the band didn't tour to promote the album.

Le Bon described the song as 'very un-Duran Duran like', 'in your face' and 'a bit rude' in a 2015 piece on DuranDuran.com. But aside from being about, in part, a 'biker' and 'metalhead' who 'break[s] heads in the Sugar Shack', there's nothing aggressive about the track itself.

Unlike many of the band's most successful songs, Le Bon tells a story about a couple – the biker and a character called China and her affair with the narrator – through lyrics that are responsible for the album's first cringeworthy moments. Following the run-in at the Sugar Shack (a possible reference to a place where a fight broke out involving the band in the early 1980s), Le Bon sings, 'We're gonna see who's gonna take who home', awkwardly rhyming 'home' with the previous line's 'stoned'. A bit later, he launches into an extended chorus consisting of the repeated line 'China, na, China, na, na, na', as if he's simply run out of words. Aside from the lyrics, the music is straightforward pop rock dominated by an organ-like keyboard riff and other odd synthesiser noises.

The video – directed by Andy Delaney and Monty Whitebloom, a duo called Big TV! – showed the new-look Duran Duran. Le Bon, his long hair now shorn close, is dressed casually in a shirt that resembles a sports jersey, and Cuccurullo, happy to show off his buff physique, doesn't have a shirt on at all. It also features a group of models in matching wigs and a gang of bikers. The clip is colourful and follows the song's storyline about China's affair, but ultimately, it's a bit generic and largely void of the band's DNA.

'Liberty' (Duran Duran)
The album gets back on track with the title song, which features jaunty keyboards and refreshingly simple lyrics. Boosted by soulful backup vocals, Le Bon addresses a lost love, singing in falsetto, 'And you can call me (if you want to stay with me) at your liberty'. In the bridge, he sings, 'Help me out. I live in doubt. Sort me out. Yeah', each brief line punctuated by a Cuccurullo riff. The song also features the album's first excellent guitar solo. The lovely track showcases a more adult contemporary sound featuring pop-oriented music and often romantic lyrics that the band pursued in the years ahead.

'Hothead' (Duran Duran)
The album goes off the rails again with 'Hothead', which features soundbites from US President George H. W. Bush and news reports from that country. The song is apparently a commentary about greed-driven, manipulative television news programmes that depict the planet as spinning out of control. Its chorus, on which Le Bon sings, 'Time, time will change the picture', is catchy. But the track and the political statement it attempts to make are ultimately dragged down by clunky lyrics like 'Watching lady, watching man' and Le Bon's attempt at rapping. As Cuccurullo noodles on guitar, Le Bon breaks into an awkward extended rap before the track comes to an abrupt close.

'Serious' (Duran Duran)
Released as a single in November 1990. Chart place: UK: 48
The album's second single is one of its better moments. Rhodes contributes the ethereal synths he's known for, and Cuccurullo adds equally atmospheric guitar. Le Bon's lyrics – including the almost laissez-faire lines 'Don't worry if

you're confused. We all tend to be sometimes. The whole world is getting used. That's just the way it is' – fit the chilled musical style perfectly.

That vibe extended to the track's recording, during which Cuccurullo stripped down to his birthday suit on his actual birthday. 'I strapped on the guitar and we got to work', the guitarist said in an online note to fans in 2019. The song's descending bassline and 'guitar pedal tone section' were then created, with Cuccurullo in the nude.

The video for the single, also directed by Big TV!, features close-up footage of model Tess Daly and the band in black and white. Shots of human circus performers and a caged 'ape' are interspersed with clips of the band members performing the song, smiling and mouthing the lyrics. During the track's shimmering instrumental bridge, colour images of the band appear distorted, as if reflected in a house of mirrors. The members seem to be having a good time, and Rhodes even appears to be chewing gum in this fitting video for a classic track.

The song is one of the few from *Liberty* to have a life after the album faded into memory. Le Bon's vocals were featured on Ferry Corsten's 2005 trance hit 'Fire', and the track was revived by Duran Duran for *MTV Unplugged* and included on their best-of album *Greatest*.

'All Along The Water' (Duran Duran)
After a high point, the album hits another low with 'All Along The Water'. Cuccurullo adds some interesting riffs and a great solo to the song, which is fine musically but fizzles out due to the repetitive, sexually suggestive lyrics. 'Playing with me like a cat', Le Bon sings. 'Scrape your fingers down my back. Pin me to the ground'. The song mostly consists of him singing variations of the line 'All along the water baby' repeatedly, which ultimately isn't very interesting.

'My Antarctica' (Duran Duran)
This sublime ballad is the album's major highlight. A piano-like keyboard riff plays throughout the track as Le Bon delivers one of his best vocal performances. Cuccurullo's 'ambient reversed guitars', Taylor's gentle bassline and Campbell's understated drumming add to the song's icy-cool sound.

The lyrics, about two lovers seeking 'time for a thousand vows, oh a thousand promises we forgot to be realised', are some of Le Bon's best as he addresses sex in a more mature manner than on some of the album's other tracks. 'We make love to make our heat', he sings in one tender yet sultry line. 'And we throb in my Antarctica'. It's even more impressive that he delivered such high-quality lyrics during a period when he often experienced writer's block.

The song is held in high esteem by the band, as evidenced by its inclusion as the B-side of the 'Ordinary World' single released years later.

'First Impression' (Duran Duran)

This song's lyrics, about 'little Johnny from the back streets of the UK' who 'loves the noise and he loves to play', are a more successful attempt at telling a story than the lead single. In the song, 'Johnny' (and perhaps the entire band) 'won't give up' or 'give in' until they get 'inside your pretty skin' – suggesting that Duran Duran still had fire in their bellies in the new decade. The up-tempo track, which opens with the words 'rock-n-roll star', spoken by Andy Warhol, features guitar heroics from Cuccurullo. The straightforward rock song, while pleasant, is a bit generic coming from a band as creative as Duran Duran. The song is also marred by Le Bon's vocals, which border on shouting rather than singing.

'Read My Lips' (Duran Duran)

Duran Duran are ready to 'rock it' again with this track – and to make it clear, they even announce it in the intro. The song, which isn't a bad tune, also has a timely title during an era when Bush famously pledged not to raise taxes in the US. Le Bon embodies a sleazy character as he sings, 'Move a little closer. Trust me I'm not on the make. That's a lie!' He's backed by powerful guitar riffs, a dynamic rhythm section and synths that add a glam rock flavour.

'Can You Deal With It' (Duran Duran)

This track, another fine moment on the album, features Le Bon looking for someone who's ready to 'blow the rules away' and 'trash these yesterdays'. It's driven by Taylor's strong bassline, Rhodes' bubbling synths and Cuccurullo's reverberating guitar riffs. The only downfall is the chorus, which is marred by Le Bon's repeated shouts of 'Can you deal with it?'

Taylor sang lead vocals on a demo version of the song, which he also later played live during his solo career in the late 1990s.

'Venice Drowning' (Duran Duran)

This atmospheric song is perhaps most notable for its lyrics, including the lines 'divine blasphemer tempting. Holy beads of jism with the scarlet catechism'. It's also a bit plodding musically and lacks a proper chorus, but the song does fit the overall lyrical style of the band since it focuses on sexual subject matter with a dark twist.

Le Bon described the track as a 'sexy zombie-vampire song', which makes it even more intriguing. In it, 'Venice' searches for a partner: 'the perfect stranger' and 'lover'. 'The body stirs and is reanimated', he speaks in the bridge, possibly about the zombie-vampire partner. 'Only briefly – but then life is very brief'. These lines are followed by a woman speaking in Italian – perhaps a shout-out to their large fanbase in that country.

'Downtown' (Duran Duran)

Duran Duran aim for an epic album closer with 'Downtown' but again fall short. As on much of the album, Cuccurullo delivers some standout guitar riffs. However, the lyrics seem uninspired, especially in the chorus, which consists only of the repeated line 'Downtown all of the way down'. The song is among the half-baked ideas that make up more than half the album, which could have been a solid EP instead.

With a relatively quick turnaround between *Big Thing* and *Liberty* and under pressure from their record company, the band clearly didn't have time to develop many musical ideas that were well thought out. (In the UK, their albums were then being released by Parlophone Records, whose name EMI had revived at the time.) Though the album has its fans, it captures a band during a period of transition, yet it ultimately paved the way for what was to come.

Extra Tracks

'Throb' (Duran Duran)

The B-side of 'Violence Of Summer' is an instrumental version of 'My Antarctica', whose title references the latter song's lyrics. 'Throb' highlights Cuccurullo's guitar work as well as the synths, which are a hallmark of the album track. This stunningly beautiful song works effectively, even without its brilliant lyrics about two lovers who 'throb' in Antarctica.

'Yo Bad Azizi' (Duran Duran)

This jarring track, one of two B-sides on the 'Serious' single, starts with a sample of Marilyn Monroe singing 'Happy birthday, Mr President' and continues with Le Bon repeatedly speaking, 'Yo bad azizi as a nuclear war'. Cuccurullo adds some blazing guitar work to the song. But it's a bit blasphemous that Le Bon reworks his own classic line from 'Is There Something I Should Know?' ('You're about as easy as a nuclear war') in such a fashion.

'Water Babies' (Duran Duran)

This perplexing track, also a B-side of 'Serious', is essentially a remix of 'All Along The Water'. Whether a song like 'All Along The Water' even needed a remix is questionable, but there are at least seven remixes of 'Violence Of Summer', which probably weren't necessary either.

Duran Duran (The Wedding Album) (1993)

Personnel:
Simon Le Bon: vocals
Nick Rhodes: keyboards
John Taylor: bass
Warren Cuccurullo: guitars
Additional musicians:
John Jones: drums, keyboards, programming
Steve Ferrone: drums and percussion
Vinnie Colaiuta: drums
Bosco: percussion
Lamya: vocals
Tessa Niles: vocals
Karen Hendrix: vocal samples on 'Drowning Man'
Jack Merigg: vocal samples on 'Drowning Man'
Milton Nascimento: vocals
Recorded at Privacy, Maison Rouge and Mountain Studios from January 1991 to January 1992
Produced by Duran Duran and John Jones
Engineer: John Jones
Record label: Parlophone/Capitol
Release date: February 1993
Highest chart places: UK: 4, US: 7
Running time: 63:34
Current edition: out of print

Duran Duran were again in flux after their first major musical flop. Becoming a five-piece band again hadn't been the magic trick they'd hoped for and perhaps even backfired.

So, almost as quickly as *Liberty* vanished from the public consciousness, Sterling Campbell disappeared from the band lineup. He reportedly left because he didn't want to relocate to London to record a new album with the rest of the band. However, according to Taylor's memoir, *In The Pleasure Groove*, their working relationship wasn't entirely harmonious. The bassist wrote of the energetic young drummer: 'He wants to run the band, too. He is telling me exactly what Simon should be doing, what Nick should be doing. He can't help himself.' Following Campbell's departure, he went on to become a member of the American rock group Soul Asylum and tour with Bowie and others.

Cuccurullo remained and became a key player, helping steer the band into one of their most successful periods. The prolonged break between *Liberty* and its follow-up – and without a tour to draw away their attention – gave them plenty of time in the studio, Privacy, which was in Cuccurullo's home in Battersea, London.

It was also a time of change for two band members on a personal level. Taylor wed Amanda de Cadenet, then 19 – 12 years younger than him – and pregnant with their child. The host of the Channel 4 television show *The Word* had been dubbed a 'wild child' by the UK tabloid press, which hounded the pair. The newlyweds fled to Los Angeles to escape the media glare, so Taylor wasn't always present for the recording sessions overseas. Meanwhile, Rhodes was going through a divorce.

Amid the changes in the band's personnel and in the members' personal lives, Duran Duran were seeking a comeback amid a vastly different musical landscape. In a scene dominated by grunge, alternative rock and hip-hop, there didn't seem to be much of an opening for the new wave sounds that they were known for. However, they forged ahead, focusing on the writing process, amassing more than a dozen solid songs and getting the mixing just right.

Indeed, the band hadn't hunkered down in a studio setting for so long a period before. Producer John Jones described the grass-roots spirit of the initial sessions at Cuccurullo's home in an interview with *Forbes* in 2023:

> He suggested that they come over and start writing at his place. That's basically where *The Wedding Album* started ... I would say [the band members] trusting each other, being able to work together in that room with one mic in the middle, all of us wearing headphones, clapping, singing, whatever – it was just so brilliant.

Ideas for the most indelible song on their second self-titled album stemmed from those sessions – the instant classic 'Ordinary World' – while others came later, like 'Come Undone', which was recorded without Taylor. Jones called The Beatles' *White Album* – another effort that featured a mix of musical styles – 'our guiding light' in the making of *The Wedding Album*. Duran Duran's LP, like The Beatles' eponymous double album, featured significant contributions from every member, but as was customary for Duran Duran, writing credits were shared among them all.

The album's nickname came from its cover art, an elegant collage of sepia-toned wedding photos of the band members' parents embossed with 'Duran Duran' in gold lettering. For the artwork, designers Nick Egan and Eric Roinestad took a DIY approach, using materials like Dymo-style labels and gold leaf. Inside, pictures of the band members taken at the University of London Students' Union photo booth were accompanied by ones from artist Dean Chamberlain, Rhodes and Taylor, as well as an 'illustration' by the keyboardist's young daughter, Tatjana. Egan, who had met Taylor at the suggestion of American actor Billy Zane and became a decades-long collaborator, has called the artwork the 'ultimate punk rock cover'. The members embraced an equally stylish image, favouring Vivienne Westwood suits – another punk rock throwback, which had become a designer fashion label – and hair colours ranging from bleach blonde to shocking purple.

They were also under new management, Left Bank, which was as keen as the members themselves for a comeback. Though the album was completed in early 1992, their record label delayed its release until 1993, perhaps a sign that the group were no longer the priority act they once were. However, that changed when the first single, 'Ordinary World', began receiving radio airplay in the US – apparently after the record company itself had leaked the track.

Duran Duran later parted ways with EMI/Capitol (now owned by Universal Music Group), and *The Wedding Album* is one of three studio albums to remain out of print, so vinyl copies regularly sell for handsome sums. But the quality and impact of the album and its wealth of B-sides and unreleased video footage from that era make it more than worthy of a deluxe reissue.

The Wedding Album era was a magical time for the band, from the spirited recording sessions to the successful attempt to relaunch their brand as unquestionably modern but undeniably Duran Duran. Their fortunes had shifted and it was all thanks to the music itself.

'Too Much Information' (Duran Duran)

Released as a single in August 1993. Chart places: UK: 35, US: 45

The album gets off to an energetic start with this guitar-driven single, which features timely and cheeky lyrics that are a commentary on mass media and even Duran Duran themselves. 'Destroyed by MTV, I hate to bite the hand that feeds me', Le Bon sings in lyrics about the 'love-hate relationship' between the band and the channel, which he describes as 'partners in crime' in the documentary *Extraordinary World*. Later in the song, he adds, 'This band is perfect just don't scratch the surface'. The track is chock-full of classic lines, including 'A COLA manufacturer is sponsoring the war' and 'Dilate your mind', which became the name of the band's world tour. The up-tempo track was a mild chart success following the album's two massive hit ballads.

The single was accompanied by a colourful video directed by Julien Temple, known for his work with The Sex Pistols. It features the band performing onstage amid the *Dilate Your Mind* tour set, complete with a giant tube of lipstick. Taylor, dressed in a blue coat and red pants, sports bright red hair. Rhodes wears a rainbow-coloured suit, his hair dyed purple and, in a delightful throwback to the 1980s, holds a keyboard as if it were a keytar. Le Bon is shown shirtless, wearing a suit of newsprint fabric or dressed in a bright pink waistcoat and silver pants. When Cuccurullo isn't shirtless, he wears a furry electric-blue coat. The audience watch the band perform through 3D glasses, perhaps to best take in the over-the-top spectacle.

The song was driven by Cuccurullo's riffs, according to Jones. 'It was one of the early ones, too, another Warren-started song', the producer told *Forbes* in 2023. With the addition of Le Bon's witty lyrics, Rhodes' dynamic synths, Taylor's driving bassline and solid drumming by Steve Ferrone, the track serves as a perfect shot of adrenaline to kick-start the album.

'Ordinary World' (Duran Duran)

Released as a single in December 1992 (US) and January 1993 (UK). Chart places: UK: 6, US: 3

The album's first single is its finest moment and arguably Duran Duran's crowning achievement.

Le Bon wrote the lyrics in memory of his late friend David Miles in an attempt to let go of his grief. 'I turned on the lights, the TV and the radio. Still I can't escape the ghost of you', Le Bon sings. 'Where is my friend when I need you most? Gone away'. But perhaps the loss of a loved one isn't quite as significant when compared to the troubles facing the world at large. 'Papers in the roadside tell of suffering and greed. Fear today, forgot tomorrow', he continues. 'Ooh, here beside the news of holy war and holy need. Ours is just a little sorrowed talk'.

The song, one of the band's first ideas for the album, features everyone on top form. Le Bon is at his best, his vocals building in intensity, leading up to the soaring outro. In addition to the outstanding vocals, Cuccurullo contributes impressive work on both acoustic and electric guitar, Rhodes and Jones add classic strings and modern synths (including an appearance by a newer Jupiter-8) and Taylor plays an understated bassline, adding a flourish towards the end of the song. The track also features Ferrone's powerful drumming.

The video, directed by Egan, embodies his vision of an extraordinary world filled with lush greenery, featuring a woman in a wedding dress and hat inspired by the Federico Fellini film *Juliet Of The Spirits*. The clip, filmed at the Huntington Botanical Gardens in San Marino, California, includes visuals from the album artwork and follows its general style, making it the ideal promotional video for the single and the LP as a whole. As the woman and the band members walk through the garden, Rhodes stops to adjust the elaborate bow across her bodice and to snap a photo. In performance clips, the band members appear in light and shadow. (Befitting a song with an epic guitar solo, Cuccurullo plays a double-necked instrument.) Their performance is projected onto a video screen along with artwork by Chamberlain. The bride watches the visuals as she reflects on the future, swaying to the music at times. Towards the end of the clip, the band members, dressed in suits, walk barefoot – a nod to the cover of The Beatles' *Abbey Road*, as well as to their own video for 'Save A Prayer'.

'Ordinary World' was a massive hit that won an Ivor Novello Award for songwriting. It has been covered by acts including Aurora and Adam Lambert, was performed by Le Bon with Luciano Pavarotti and was featured in the film *Layer Cake*. Above all, it remains a timeless musical statement.

'Love Voodoo' (Duran Duran)

The album goes from serious to sultry with 'Love Voodoo'. This bass-driven track features Lamya, the Soul II Soul vocalist who toured with Duran Duran, took a star turn on their episode of *MTV Unplugged* and recorded as a solo artist before her untimely death from a heart attack at the age of 45.

Le Bon's lyrics address a 'queen of sensuality' who 'peel[s] me like an onion skin' and 'shelter[s] me from Liberty' – a reference to the ill-fated album. Later, he turns the tables, singing, 'But I'm content to compromise until the day you realise that I have been manipulating you'. The track also features Cuccurullo's understated acoustic strumming and a cool vocal breakdown leading up to the bridge.

Rhodes has called the song 'a twisted love story'. That and the title's reference to voodoo were enough for the band to re-record it with Cuccurullo for their Halloween-themed album, *Danse Macabre*, on which it is titled 'Love Voudou'.

'Drowning Man' (Duran Duran)

This up-tempo dance track features a piano-like keyboard intro, grinding guitar riffs and a throbbing drum beat. A single version was released that included remixes of the song, aimed at dance clubs in the US.

Le Bon returns to a favourite topic, mass media, and references America: 'Gun in his pocket and a heart of ham, Uncle Sam', a personification of the US government. In the lyrics, this character threatens to drag everyone down with him, and as Le Bon chants in the bridge: 'Infect us all with his TV screen'. While the song features some interesting guitar work, the odd juxtaposition of lyrics that seem to be a political statement and upbeat dance music makes it one of the album's less impressive tracks.

'Shotgun' (Duran Duran)

This short song serves as a bridge between the dance-oriented 'Drowning Man' and the sensual 'Come Undone'. It features brief vocals by Le Bon, guitar riffs from Cuccurullo and the sound of a gun being fired, referring to the song's title, as well as to the previous mention of a gun on the LP (and given the *White Album* inspiration, possibly even a nod to The Beatles' 'Happiness Is A Warm Gun'). 'Shotgun' also harks back to Paul McCartney's 'Wild Honey Pie', also from the *White Album*, as both songs are the fifth track on their respective LPs and widely viewed as filler material. But despite the Duran Duran song's weak points, it's hard to imagine *The Wedding Album* without it.

'Come Undone' (Duran Duran)

Released as a single in March 1993. Chart places: UK: 13, US: 7

This self-produced track, a late addition to the album, is essentially a duet between Le Bon and singer Tessa Niles. The guitars are inspired by 'First Impression' from *Liberty*, though the two songs aren't very similar.

The LP's second single, built around Cuccurullo's distinctive guitar hook and a drum loop, had been planned for a side project with Rhodes and Bush singer Gavin Rossdale, according to the book *Notorious* by Steve Malins. But when Le Bon heard the song, he promptly added a melody and lyrics – a birthday gift for his wife, Yasmin. 'Signed with a home tattoo', he sings. 'Happy birthday to you was created for you'. The track also features other classic Le Bon lines like 'It'll take a little time, might take a little crime to come undone'. Like 'Ordinary World', his lyrics are personal and deeply sincere, and therefore, among his best.

The video, also directed by Temple, features a host of people coming undone, including a child who appears to catch her parents making love, an alcoholic woman, a cross-dressing man and an elderly couple who sit together on a bench amid rising floodwaters. The water theme runs throughout the video, which also features the band performing at the London Aquarium and a woman submerged in water who breaks free of the chains that bind her. The clip, another visually stunning effort, even includes a reference to their New Romantic roots, as Le Bon and Taylor wear white shirts with ruffled collars and cuffs.

Though Taylor appears in the video, he wasn't present for the recording of the song, which features synth bass in his place. It's widely believed that the track's drum loop samples the song 'Ashley's Roachclip' by The Soul Searchers, but Duran Duran have stated that it doesn't.

'Breath After Breath' (Duran Duran and Milton Nascimento)
This uplifting song is the first Duran Duran track to feature a high-profile guest vocalist. Brazilian singer Milton Nascimento co-wrote the song and appeared in the video, part of which was filmed at the Iguazú Falls near the border of his home country and Argentina.

The song is inspired by world music with its flamenco-style acoustic guitars, drums from Vinnie Colaiuta and percussion by Bosco. Le Bon sings mostly in a lower register, reserving the highest notes for the Brazilian tenor and his distinctive falsetto.

The video, directed by Keith Ward, features the band performing onstage, footage of Le Bon, Nascimento and Rhodes (with a typewriter) in front of a scenic waterfall and additional shots of Taylor and Cuccurullo. Nascimento's lyrics, translated from Portuguese into English, appear as if typewritten onscreen. The clip features the members smiling and in high spirits, befitting the song's joyful nature.

'UMF' (Duran Duran)
The band members embrace their funkier side on this catchy track. Le Bon combines a hip-hop-style delivery at times and a Prince-esque falsetto at others. 'A to Z, she's doin' it to my head', he sings in one of his best vocal performances on the album. 'We don't need to go to bed, you'll find, to make love to the ultimate mind'. The soaring vocals, as well as the upbeat guitars and keyboards, build towards the track's conclusion. As it fades out, the band members' clapping can be heard – yet another parallel with the *White Album*, on which 'The Continuing Story Of Bungalow Bill' also ends in applause.

'Femme Fatale' (Lou Reed)
This late addition to the album, which was produced by the band, is a tribute to one of their musical heroes. Duran Duran had earlier shared the stage with Lou Reed and later impressed him with another cover of one of his songs.

On 'Femme Fatale', which was released as a single in France, Le Bon adds a male perspective to The Velvet Underground track, which was originally sung by Nico. Duran Duran step up the tempo a bit from the dreamlike original, their version featuring Cuccurullo's heavy guitar riffs late in the track and Ferrone's live percussion. Like almost all the band's cover versions, they add their own twist. Le Bon delivers a spoken-word bridge and sings it in a way that Nico or Reed himself couldn't have done.

The striking black-and-white video, directed by photographer Ellen von Unwerth, shows the band members in a car as they encounter a stunning femme fatale outside. This seductive woman lures them into a nightclub filled with other beautiful creatures, some of whom appear to be dressed in drag. The clip ends with a now-classic image of the four band members lying in a circle as rose petals fall over them, which was later used inside the *Thank You* album.

'None Of The Above' (Duran Duran)
This rock-driven track, a highlight on the album, features guitar at every turn, as well as killer lyrics and vocals. Le Bon, an agnostic, references 'money', 'power' and 'holy roads' in the song. 'God knows where I'm going to', he ponders. 'It's a lonely burning question'. Ultimately, he determines that 'when it comes down to my soul, freedom puts my faith in none of the above'. While the lyrics raise serious questions about faith, the brilliant melody and high-energy music make the track one of the band's most infectious. It shares a possible lyrical theme with 'New Religion' and, like that classic song, is entirely Duran Duran – but with a modern edge.

The album didn't yield a proper fourth single in the UK or the US, but 'None Of The Above' would have been a great candidate. It was only released as a single in Japan.

'Shelter' (Duran Duran)
On this track, Le Bon sings in falsetto to the subject, a woman he sees 'working this vicious road' who's 'looking beat and cold'. 'Money or reputation doesn't mean a thing to me', he continues. 'Special communication it's the only thing we need'. The keyboard-driven track features arpeggiated synths, which, along with the vocals, make this another standout effort on the album's second half. The song also exists as a slowed-down demo, which was wisely sped up and pumped up to produce the final album track.

'To Whom It May Concern' (Duran Duran)
This song opens with the sound of a phone being dialled before Le Bon addresses a 'Mr. Bones', as he sings, 'You can try to pull us down with your

pin-stripe weasel stuff, but word travels in this town'. He continues, 'You said, 'Boys, I'll get you more, but you've got to pay me by the hour', noting that this shady character (or characters, given the band's past managerial associations) also 'ate my royalties'. In addition to the powerful lyrics, which no doubt struck a chord with a band who had encountered plenty of unscrupulous characters over the years, the music is fantastic. It builds into the outro, which features chunky guitar riffs and a funky bassline and leads seamlessly into the album's final track.

'Sin Of The City' (Duran Duran)

Arguably, this is the band's most epic album closer, beginning with the sounds of an urban streetscape before the tale is told of the deadly Happy Land fire set by an arsonist at an unlicensed club in the Bronx in 1990. Though Le Bon sings, 'The sin is that 89 died', there were actually 87 victims, most of them Honduran Americans. Taylor, who reportedly wrote the majority of the lyrics, also later sang the song with his own band, John Taylor Terroristen.

While the track essentially tells the story of a real-life event, it's also a commentary on injustice. Though the fire chief branded Happy Land a fire hazard and ordered it to close – with Le Bon singing, 'No one ever paid him no mind' – the owners flouted the law in order to remain in business and continue making money off unsuspecting patrons. The lyrics are hard-hitting: 'Just one firecracker on a big bonfire of self-serving penny-pinching wiseguy style. Never allowing for the human condition'.

Amid synths that sound like fierce flames at times and incendiary guitar riffs, Taylor delivers a driving bassline that's one of his best on the album. The song's heavy topic doesn't prevent the band from offering yet another earworm of a chorus. The final minute of the track is reserved for more fantastic guitar work from Cuccurullo, who brings the album to a close in much the same way it started on 'Too Much Information'. More than anything, *The Wedding Album* is a showcase for the band's songwriting talents, which were sparked by sessions in the guitarist's own living room.

Extra Tracks

'Stop Dead' (Duran Duran)

Like all the band's best musical efforts, *The Wedding Album* also has terrific B-sides. A trio of extra tracks were included on a UK tour edition of the album, and one of them, 'Stop Dead', was featured as the B-side on the US CD single for 'Come Undone'. The song, with its funky guitar, catchy chorus and keyboard riff, is strong musically but a bit thin lyrically, which may be why it didn't make the cut for the album. However, it's still a fun track, with lyrics that offer a mix of driving metaphors and sexual innuendo. 'I hit the brake. I must be dreaming', Le Bon sings about a potential love interest. 'Stop dead in my tracks. Got to fix on you'.

'Time For Temptation' (Duran Duran)
This track, the B-side on the US cassette single of 'Come Undone', features jaunty keyboards, fuzzy guitar riffs and profound lyrics. Le Bon again references religion as he sings about 'a slave for promotion to the afterlife'. 'Why you chasing a lost religion of guilty feelings that belong in yesterday?' he asks the subject, who he warns could be whipped 'into shape' by those who wield 'the cross like a gun'. While the lyrics in the verses are strong, the song peters out towards the end with the repetition of its two-line chorus.

'Falling Angel' (Duran Duran)
The best B-side of the bunch is featured on another version of the US CD single for 'Come Undone'. 'Falling Angel' (sometimes referred to as 'Fallen Angel') is a soaring song that's strong enough to have made the album.

The track opens with Taylor's chunky bass riff before Cuccurullo's guitars kick in. The song, with excellent lyrics and vocals by Le Bon and shimmering synths from Rhodes, is among the band's best non-album tracks. Le Bon sings in the character of a falling angel 'dangl[ing] in the blue' who seemingly longs for earthly pleasures. 'It's my time all I have for my crime is such. Knowing that the thing I love is that which I can't touch', he sings. He closes the track by repeatedly singing, 'I don't believe it all. But I believe in you'.

As with 'Like An Angel' – a similarly named track that also didn't make it onto an album released during a golden era for the band – 'Falling Angel' is a testament to their ability to write quality songs, especially when they're at the top of their game.

Thank You (1995)

Personnel:
Simon Le Bon: vocals
Nick Rhodes: keyboards
John Taylor: bass
Warren Cuccurullo: guitars
Additional musicians:
Roger Taylor: drums
Terry Bozzio: drums
Steve Ferrone: drums
Tony Thompson: drums
Abe Laboriel Jr.: drums on 'Lay Lady Lay' and 'I Wanna Take You Higher Again'
Anthony J. Resta: programming, drums on 'White Lines', 'Lay Lady Lay', '911 Is A Joke', 'Ball Of Confusion', 'I Wanna Take You Higher Again'
John Jones: programming
Mark Tinley: programming
Grandmaster Flash and the Furious Five with Melle Mel: vocals
Lamya: vocals on 'White Lines', 'I Wanna Take You Higher', 'Drive By'
Curtis King Jr.: vocals on 'I Wanna Take You Higher'
Tessa Niles: vocals on 'Perfect Day' and 'Watching The Detectives'
Maxayn Lewis: vocals on 'Ball Of Confusion'
Flo & Eddie (Mark Volman and Howard Kaylan): vocals on 'Success'
Lee Oskar: harmonica
Jonathan Elias: Moog
Bruce Dukov: violin
Ron Folsom: violin
Armen Garabedian: violin
Henry Ferber: violin
Berj Garabedian: violin
Joy Lyle: violin
Michelle Kikuchi Richards: violin
Maria Newman: violin
Pamela Goldsmith: viola
Scott Haupert: viola
Suzie Katayama: cello
Recorded at Privacy and around the world from 1992 to 1994
Produced by Duran Duran with John Jones, Anthony J. Resta and Bob St. John
Engineers: Ken Scott, John Jones, Tony Taverner, Avril McCintosh, Steve Churchyard, Anthony J. Resta, Bob St. John
Record label: Parlophone/Capitol
Release date: March 1995
Chart places: UK: 12, US: 19
Running time: 54:26
Current edition: out of print

Following *The Wedding Album*, Duran Duran were back at the height of their powers. They were honoured with an Ivor Novello Award and a star on the Hollywood Walk of Fame and embarked on a world tour with high-profile opening acts, including The Cranberries and Terence Trent D'Arby. They played reimagined versions of their newest hits and classic songs on *MTV Unplugged,* incorporating these acoustic tracks into their elaborate live shows, which featured a string section.

All the while, the band planned their next move: a covers album to be released while they were still riding high after the success of their previous album. But in Duran Duran's world (aka 'Durantime'), things don't always go as planned. Le Bon tore a vocal cord, forcing the tour to be postponed for weeks and leading to some dates being cancelled altogether. The recording of their covers album turned into a huge production that involved scores of additional musicians and sessions in studios around the world, including at Prince's Paisley Park in Minnesota and a mobile studio in the south of France. The situation harked back to the strained sessions for *Seven And The Ragged Tiger*.

Once again, Duran Duran were one of the biggest bands in the world and, along with their 1980s contemporaries like U2 and INXS, had now managed to establish themselves in the new decade. They all lived like rock stars, too, as Le Bon told *The Guardian* in 2003:

> We were finishing *Thank You* at Nick's house in France, and I went to stay at Michael Hutchence's place nearby. Michael and Bono and I were in this thing called the Lead Singers Club. For a couple of months in the summer of 1994, we lived it up in the south of France. Michael took drugs, but he had a good relationship with his girlfriend [model Helena Christensen] at the time. He certainly wasn't suicidal or fucking up really badly. The club's main meeting place was Nick's swimming pool.

However, while U2 and INXS were each releasing albums of original material, Duran Duran were mining other artists' work for the follow-up to one of their most successful albums. The music press, as if they could smell blood in the water, were ready to give the band and their new LP a critical lashing.

Duran Duran decided to take on some of the most revered songs in rock, including Led Zeppelin's 'Thank You', Lou Reed's 'Perfect Day' and Bob Dylan's 'Lay Lady Lay'. But in a wrongheaded move, they also chose to remake the hip-hop classic '911 Is A Joke' by Public Enemy and included not one but two versions of 'I Wanna Take You Higher' by Sly and the Family Stone on the album. Half of the LP, including the rock ballads, is pretty good, but that wasn't enough to please the critics, who lambasted the album. Even more than ten years after the release of *Thank You*, *Q* magazine unceremoniously named it the worst album of all time.

The album cover, designed by artist Eric Roinestad, is a silver-toned collage featuring images of the artists covered by the band. The covers of the LP's singles, which feature pop art of ice cream treats and other images, are also used in the album liner notes, along with photos of the band taken by Ellen von Unwerth. *Thank You* is currently out of print.

The mid-1990s turned out to be a time of both exhilarating success and profound change for the band. Taylor entered rehab for the first time, planting the seeds for his journey towards finally getting clean. Duran Duran were about to embark on their wilderness years, during which they recorded some fantastic music but became increasingly distanced from what made them who they were.

However, first, there was *Thank You*, and the title said it all. While the album wasn't the commercial or critical success the band had hoped for, it was still meant as a heartfelt tribute to many of their musical heroes and others who had inspired them over the years.

'White Lines (Don't Do It)' (Melvin Glover, Sylvia Robinson)
Released as a single in June 1995. Chart place: UK: 17
The band's version of the hip-hop smash by Melle Mel and Grandmaster Flash, which features the original artists and the Furious Five, was only a mild chart success in the UK but ended up having immense staying power.

Their reimagining of the track is aided by Cuccurullo's riffs and the iconic bassline, played here by Taylor, who told *Complex Magazine* in 2012 that they aimed to 'do a killer version' of the song. Along with urban-edged synths, the song incorporated rap rock sounds, which predated that genre's rise in popularity in the late 1990s. It has become a staple in their live shows.

The original version of the song also had legs due to pop culture references that have kept it in the zeitgeist, including its inclusion in films like *Cocaine Bear* and *Shaun Of The Dead*, in which the main characters drunkenly sing it on the way home from the Winchester pub.

The video, directed by Nick Egan and featuring appearances by Grandmaster Flash, Melle Mel and the Furious Five, opens with Taylor rubbing his nose – and the drug references don't stop there. The video features white powder galore, as well as record-scratching and break-dancing. The band members are dressed in black as they perform in a white-walled room. Le Bon kicks and spits water at the camera and otherwise hams it up, almost as if he's dipped into the 'white lines' himself.

The high-energy track features an incendiary guitar solo from Cuccurullo, drums by Steve Ferrone and drum loops from Anthony J. Resta. Thankfully, the rapping is left mostly to the rappers.

'I Wanna Take You Higher' (Sylvester Stewart)
The first version of this Sly and the Family Stone classic to appear on the album proves that one iteration would have been more than enough.

Nevertheless, the band's spirited version includes Cuccurullo's heavy riffs, Taylor's driving bass and Chic's Tony Thompson on drums. But the track starts to fizzle out as Lamya interjects, 'You said you were gonna take me somewhere. (Higher!) Oh, yeah! I'm down with that'. Chants of 'Go Charlie! Go Charlie' (a reference to Le Bon's nickname) by background vocalists, including Grandmaster Flash and the Furious Five, follow. It's only then that the sound of a harmonica, which was prominently featured throughout the original version of the song, finally kicks in.

'Perfect Day' (Lou Reed)
Released as a single in March 1995. Chart place: UK: 28
This sublime version of Lou Reed's classic track features drummer Roger Taylor back in the fold for the first time in a decade. It was a minor chart success in the UK.

To accompany the album and its first single, and perhaps to try to head off expected flak from critics, the band released an electronic press kit, which featured many of the original artists sharing their thoughts about the cover versions. Reed was especially praiseworthy of 'Perfect Day':

> I think Duran Duran's version of 'Perfect Day' is possibly the best rerecording of a song of mine. I'm not sure that I sing as well as Simon sang it. I think he sings it better than I do. If I could've sung it the way he did, I would've. It wasn't for lack of trying. They recorded it the way I meant it.

Indeed, the song is one of the best on the album. The lyrics have been interpreted as being about heroin, and Reed's version was even featured in the film *Trainspotting*. Duran Duran's cover stays true to the original, which masks any darker undertones with its lines about drinking 'sangria in the park' and feeding 'animals in the zoo'. At the end of the song, the lyrical intent becomes more ambiguous with the repetition of the line, 'You're gonna reap just what you sow'. The song features Le Bon's dreamy vocals, layers of synths, a lovely sitar solo by Cuccurullo and Taylor's understated drumming.

The video, another visually stunning effort from Egan, shows the band and Taylor performing in colourful suits and with bare feet inside a room that resembles a padded cell. But in their usual fashion, the space is pristine, with red walls, a neon 'Duran Duran' sign, glittering lights and a video screen. The band members appear to go insane as John Taylor crawls on all fours and Rhodes throws flowers at the camera when he's not admiring his reflection in a mirrored compact or checking his watch. Gloomy images, including skulls and withering flowers, interspersed throughout the clip, also suggest that things aren't so perfect.

'Watching The Detectives' (Elvis Costello)
Duran Duran's version of this new wave classic with a reggae beat is the second track on *Thank You* to feature Roger Taylor. Le Bon's standout vocals

add a sultry side to Costello's quirky lyrics, resulting in another highlight on the album. He adds drama to Costello's words that reference a woman who is seemingly fascinated with film noir, literally 'watching the detectives'. In the chorus, Cuccurullo punctuates each line with guitar. The song also features harmonica and a range of effects, including a door-knocking sound. Overall, it's a pleasant take on the original.

'Lay Lady Lay' (Bob Dylan)
The album's high point comes with Duran Duran's reimagining of a Dylan classic, which the songwriter himself said 'beats mine by a country mile'. The track was a single in Italy and Spain.

Duran Duran's version adds a 'Come Undone'-esque guitar riff, ambient synths and African-style percussion to the Dylan tune. Le Bon reaches into the depths of his register for his take on the tender lyrics, singing, 'Stay lady stay. Stay with your man a while', before launching into the soaring bridge. 'Don't wait any longer for your world to begin', he sings. 'You can have your cake and eat it, too'. Le Bon's suave delivery results in a more welcoming invitation than Dylan's, which may be why the singer offered such high praise for the cover. Le Bon also adds a vocal flourish at the end reminiscent of 'Ordinary World'.

Indeed, Duran Duran's 'Lay Lady Lay' combines the best of both 'Come Undone' and 'Ordinary World' – producer Jones' intention – with the classic lyrics, which Le Bon more than makes his own.

'911 Is A Joke' (Keith Shocklee, Eric Sadler, William Drayton)
The album takes a terribly wrong turn with the band's remake of this Public Enemy hit. Duran Duran's version combines Le Bon's rapping (a style which has been described as 'dad rap') with country western-style instrumentation and strange, high-pitched vocal samples. The track was heavily changed at the mixing stage, which resulted in a final version that didn't sound much like Duran Duran at all. Indeed, even Flavor Flav's stamp of approval couldn't help this train wreck of a track.

The song, which is about paramedics' poor response to emergency calls in an African American neighbourhood, is a puzzling selection for a white English rock band to cover. Comedian John Oliver accurately and humorously summed up this atrocity when he said, 'You haven't heard that disaffected anthem properly until you have heard it performed by a white man named Simon from Hertfordshire.'

'Success' (Iggy Pop, David Bowie, Ricky Gardiner)
The album gets back on track with this campy version of a song originally sung by Pop and co-written by Bowie. It's a choice of cover that, like 'Perfect Day' before it, made perfect sense for a band heavily influenced by glam rock. The Stooges' frontman himself praised Duran Duran's version.

The song begins with drums played by Terry Bozzio of Missing Persons and builds from there. Le Bon sounds more like Bowie than Pop as he delivers over-the-top lyrics like 'I'm gonna crash my car. I'm gonna wear a dress'. The track is a fun version that, like the original, doesn't take itself too seriously.

'Crystal Ship' (The Doors)

Duran Duran take on another titan of rock, The Doors, with this classic, which listeners have speculated is about drugs but is more often described as a love song about leaving a lover before departing for a tour ('The crystal ship is being filled. A thousand girls, a thousand thrills' and 'When we get back, I'll drop a line').

The highlight of Duran Duran's version is Le Bon's vocals, which channel Jim Morrison and his rich baritone. The instrumentation is fairly straightforward, which is refreshing amid a number of heavily produced and mixed tracks. The song again features Ferrone on drums.

Le Bon and Cuccurullo also performed an excellent acoustic version of the song live during the *Thank You* era.

'Ball Of Confusion' (Norman Whitfield, Barrett Strong)

This version of the Temptations' r&b classic isn't the first cover of the song by a British band, but it's the least successful, as a version by Love and Rockets released in 1986 is much better. It's a questionable selection for Duran Duran to have covered at all, let alone changed so drastically. The track features heavy bass and drums and an overarching sound effect that's difficult to pin down. Again, it's also awkward to hear lyrics about racial strife being delivered by a white singer.

Le Bon and Rhodes have acknowledged that the band probably shouldn't have touched the song. 'The original is such a definitive version that we probably should not have attempted to change it so radically', they told 'Ask Katy' on DuranDuran.com in 2008.

'Thank You' (Jimmy Page, Robert Plant)

Duran Duran redeem themselves with the title track, one of the album's best songs, which was also deemed exceptional by Led Zeppelin's Page. It also made perfect sense that a band from Birmingham would pay tribute to other musicians with shared ties to the West Midlands.

Cuccurullo adds his own flair to Page's classic riffs, and Le Bon shines in his delivery of Plant's tender vocals. In the chorus, Le Bon harmonises with himself, giving his unique take on the original, which featured both Page and Plant. Jonathan Elias and Rhodes brilliantly reimagine John Paul Jones' organ solo for the song's shimmering, Moog- and synth-soaked outro. The track also features outstanding drumming from Bozzio.

Edited versions of the song appeared on *Encomium: A Tribute To Led Zeppelin* and the soundtrack of the film *With Honors*.

'Drive By' (Duran Duran)

Duran Duran make yet another audacious move on an album chock-full of them by covering one of their own songs. 'Drive By' – an updated version of 'The Chauffeur' – features new lyrics spoken by Le Bon and standout vocals from Lamya. She adds a Middle Eastern flair to the classic line 'Sing blue silver' before lush strings and the ocarina solo, well-known from the original version, kick in. Bozzio once again plays drums.

The song lays bare the excesses of mid-1990s Duran Duran. The original was a Le Bon and Rhodes production, but the remake features a cast of musicians, including an 11-member string section. Unfortunately, quantity doesn't equal quality, as 'The Chauffeur' is a far superior song.

'I Wanna Take You Higher Again' (Sylvester Stewart)

Perplexingly, Duran Duran revisit the Sly Stone song, and perhaps this simpler version should have been the only one to make the cut. It closes the album, fading out to end one of the band's most uneven LPs. Perhaps it would have been better to close with 'Drive By', which is pretentious yet still pleasant. The band's second version of the classic track features a hi-hat reminiscent of U2's 'Mysterious Ways' and the relaxed atmosphere of the original, but its placement as the album's final track is questionable.

Extra Tracks

'The Needle And The Damage Done' (Neil Young)

The band's version of this Neil Young classic, a B-side on the 'Perfect Day' single, is good enough to have made the album. Perhaps its theme was the reason it didn't make the final cut, as it's another song about drug use. However, the track, with its melancholic vocals, understated synths and acoustic guitar, is stunning yet simplistic, so it doesn't really fit in with the rest of the heavily mixed album.

The band also nearly completed a version of Young's 'Heart Of Gold' but abandoned it around the mixing stage.

'Diamond Dogs' (Bowie)

This excellent cover would have been a welcome addition to the album as well but was only included as a bonus track on the Japanese release. Perhaps Bowie's contribution to 'Success' (he was also the producer of Reed's 'Perfect Day') and the fact that the band had covered Bowie before were the reasons they excluded the track.

As on all the band's covers of Bowie songs, they shine on 'Diamond Dogs'. They stay true to the original while adding their own touch with Rhodes' synths. Le Bon embodies Bowie's 'Halloween Jack', who's 'a real cool cat'. 'Sashay on the boardwalk', he snarls. 'Scurry to the ditch'.

The band also considered including covers of Bowie's 'We Are The Dead' and T. Rex's 'Jeepster' (reportedly with Roger Taylor), as well as Alice

Cooper's 'Elected'. The cast-off covers make one wonder what could have been.

However, Duran Duran were clearly set on taking a less conventional approach to their covers album, and the risks didn't pay off. The LP sold fewer copies than its predecessor, leaving the band at a crossroads once again.

Above: A promotional photo of the 'Fab Five' circa the release of 'The Wild Boys' in 1984. (*Mike Owen/Alamy*)

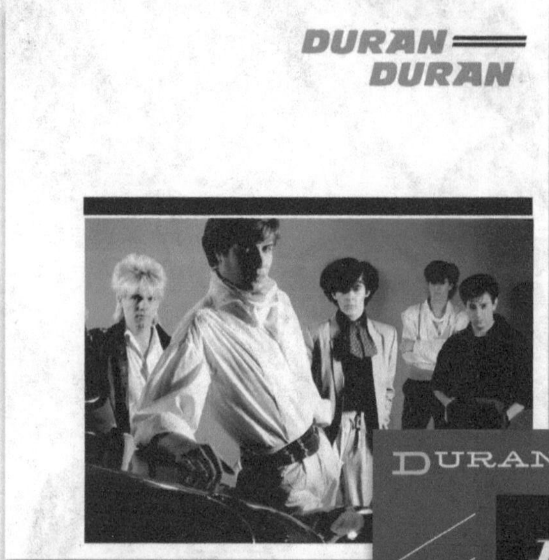

Left: The band were photographed by Fin Costello for the cover of *Duran Duran* (1981). (*Warner Music*)

Right: *Rio* (1982), Duran Duran's seminal album, features a painting on its cover by artist Patrick Nagel. (*Warner Music*)

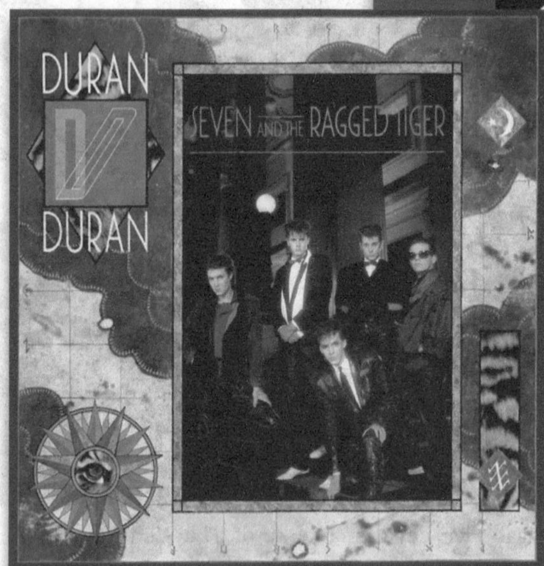

Left: The cover of *Seven And The Ragged Tiger* (1983) was designed by Malcolm Garrett. (*Warner Music*)

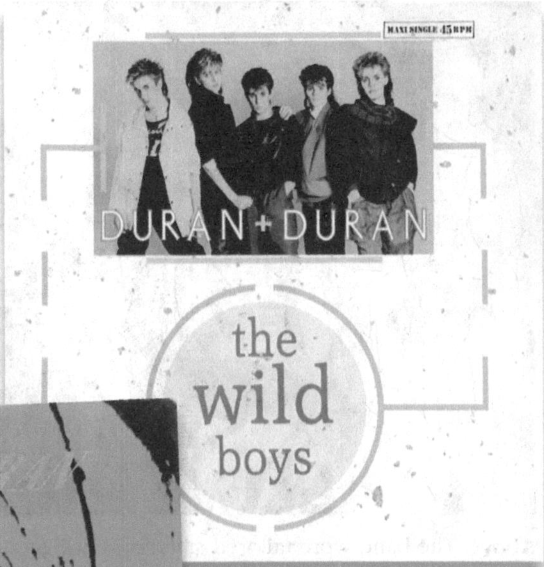

Right: 'The Wild Boys' was released in several versions, including sleeves showing the members individually and as a group. (*Warner Music*)

Left: 'A View To A Kill' is the only *James Bond* theme to reach the top of the *Billboard* charts. (*Warner Music*)

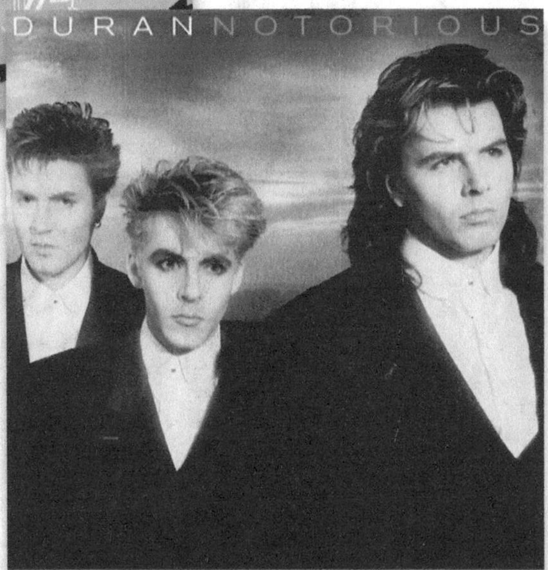

Right: *Notorious* (1986) featured a slimmed-down lineup, as only Le Bon, Rhodes and John Taylor had returned to the fold. (*Warner Music*)

Above: The band wore tailored suits from designer Antony Price for this promo portrait in 1983. (*Fin Costello/Redferns*).

Below: Duran Duran remained a five-piece band until 1985, after which both Roger and Andy Taylor left the group. (*Alamy*)

Above: Rhodes with producer Nile Rodgers during the recording of 'The Wild Boys' at Maison Rouge Studios in 1984. (*Virginia Turbett/Redferns*)

Below: Princess Diana meets the members of Duran Duran at the Prince's Trust gala in London on 20 July 1983. (*Getty Images*)

Left: John Taylor and Le Bon in the 'Planet Earth' video, the band's first, directed by Russell Mulcahy.

Right: The band embraced a New Romantic image in 1981, as seen in this still from the 'Planet Earth' video.

Left: A close-up of Le Bon from the racy 'Girls On Film' video, directed by Godley & Creme.

Right: Duran Duran perform 'The Wild Boys', a number-two hit in the UK and the US, on *Top Of The Pops* in 1984.

Left: The 'Save A Prayer' video, directed by Mulcahy, features scenes at a temple and an ancient rock fortress in Sri Lanka.

Right: John Taylor strums a guitar in this beach scene from the 'Save A Prayer' video.

Left: *Big Thing* (1988), with artwork by Hans Arnold, was their first LP since *Rio* not to feature the band on its cover. (*Warner Music*)

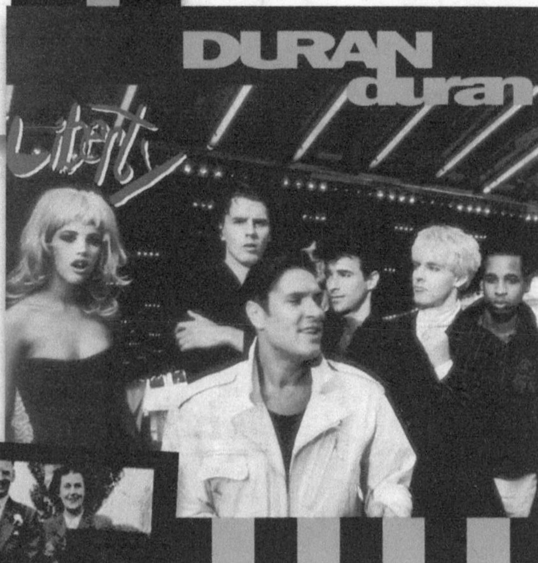

Right: Duran Duran, with new members Warren Cuccurullo and Sterling Campbell, were a five-man band again for *Liberty* (1990). (*Warner Music*)

Left: The cover of *Duran Duran* (*The Wedding Album*) includes the wedding photos of the four band members' parents. (*Warner Music*)

Right: The artwork for *Thank You* (1995) features a collage of artists whose songs Duran Duran covered for the album. (*Warner Music*)

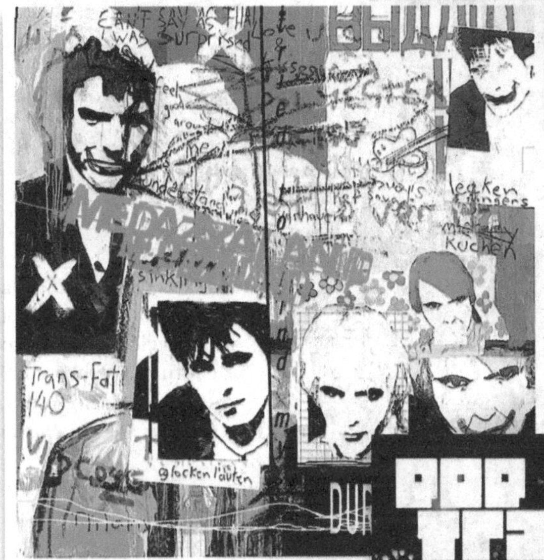

Left: *Medazzaland* (1997), with its cover artwork by Andrew Day, reflected a time of transition after John Taylor's departure. (*BMG*)

Right: *Pop Trash* (2000) was the band's last album featuring Cuccurullo until he worked with them again in 2023. (*BMG*)

Above: The band, in a 1993 promo photo, shot in a service elevator to capture a 'gritty vibe' during the grunge era. (*Karen Mason-Blair*)

Left: Duran Duran on the red carpet before their opening night performance at The Fashion Cafe in New York in 1995. (*Adam Nadel/The Associated Press*)

Above: Le Bon and Rhodes arrive at the MTV Europe Music Awards in Rome in November 2004. (*Alessandra Tarantino/The Associated Press*)

Right: Le Bon and Rhodes at Live 8 in Rome, one in a string of benefit concerts held in July 2005. (*Alessandra Tarantino/The Associated Press*)

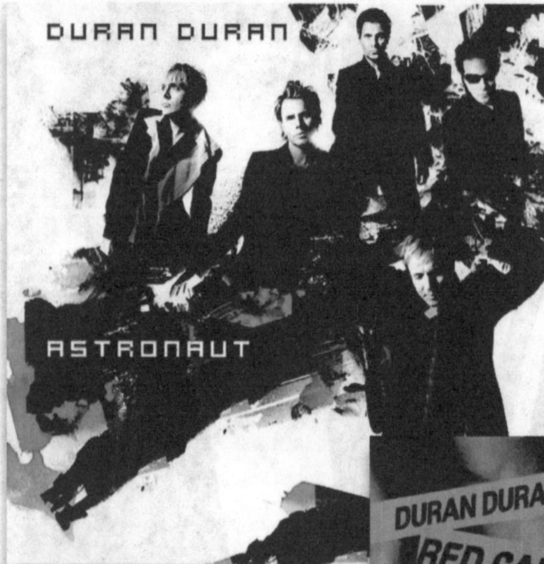

Left: The classic lineup reunited in 2001, releasing an album of new music, *Astronaut* (2004). (*BMG*)

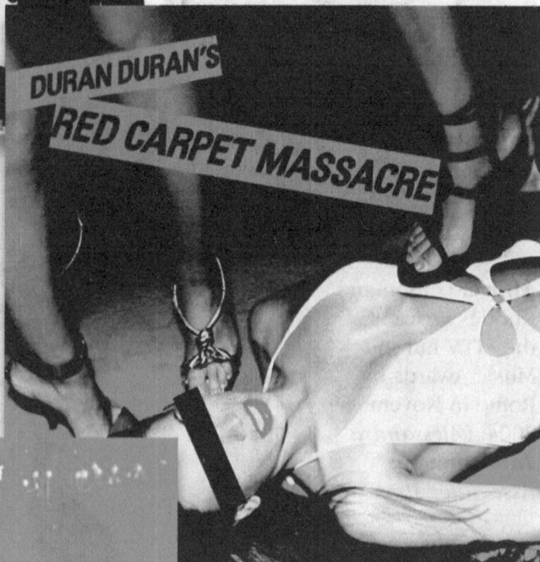

Right: *Red Carpet Massacre* (2007), the reunited lineup's first album without Andy Taylor, was co-produced by Timbaland, Justin Timberlake and Nate Hills. (*BMG*)

Left: *All You Need Is Now* (2011), co-produced by Mark Ronson, represented a return to form for the band. (*BMG*)

Right: *Paper Gods* (2015) was the band's first studio album in more than 20 years to reach the *Billboard* top ten. (*Warner Music*)

Left: *Future Past* (2021) is among a string of latter-day Duran Duran albums to hit the UK top five. (*BMG*)

Right: *Danse Macabre* (2023) includes covers, reimaginings of their own songs and new tracks. (*Tape Modern/BMG*)

Left: Le Bon performing in 2024. That year, he was awarded an MBE for services to music and charity. (*Christopher Windle*)

Below: Taylor and Le Bon join Ronson onstage during the Lovebox Festival at Victoria Park in London in July 2010. (*Gus Stewart/ Redferns*)

Above: Duran Duran in a promotional photo from 2015. They were inducted into the Rock & Roll Hall of Fame in 2022. (*Stephanie Pistel*)

Below: In 2023, the band teamed up with director Jonas Åkerlund for the 'Black Moonlight' video, in which they attend a 'seance'.

Left: The 1984 documentary *Sing Blue Silver* was a popular release on videotape, LaserDisc and, later, DVD. (*Warner Music*)

Below: An array of Duran Duran badges from the *Rio* era through *All You Need Is Now*. (*Karen Windle*)

Medazzaland (1997)

Personnel:
Simon Le Bon: vocals
Nick Rhodes: keyboards, vocals, synth bass
Warren Cuccurullo: guitars, bass, synth bass, vocals
Additional musicians:
John Taylor: bass
Steve Alexander: drums
Anthony J. Resta: drums, programming, mixing
Mark Tinley: programming
Dave DiCenso: drums
Tim Garland: saxophone
Talvin Singh: tabla and santoor
Jake Shapiro: cello
Ustad Sultan Khan: sarangi sample
Sally Stapleton: vocals
Madeleine Farley: vocals on 'Silva Halo'
Mayko Cuccurullo: vocal effects
Clem Burke: drum fill
Recorded at Privacy, Metropolis Studios, Sound Techniques, Bopnique, Long View Farm Studios, Crescent Moon Studios and A&M Studios from 1995 to 1997
Produced by TV Mania with associate producer Simon Le Bon for Syn Pro Tokyo
Additional production by Anthony J. Resta and Bob St. John
Engineers: Mark Tinley and Bob St. John
Record label: Capitol/BMG
Release date: October 1997 (US) and March 2021 (UK)
Highest chart place: UK: did not chart, US: 58
Running time: 53:17
Current edition: 2022 BMG CD/LP

After the commercial and critical disappointment of *Thank You*, Duran Duran were about to enter their most experimental phase. Electronica was on the upswing, and the band decided to pursue their version of the increasingly popular genre while including nods to their past influences. After all, their motto at the time was 'Styles change. Style doesn't.'

After a brief tour to support *Thank You*, the band members gathered for the initial recording sessions for the new album at Privacy. Meanwhile, Taylor had become part of a supergroup overseas. Neurotic Outsiders, which got their start at the Viper Room in Los Angeles, also included Steve Jones of The Sex Pistols and Duff McKagan and Matt Sorum of Guns N' Roses. They recorded a self-titled album and briefly toured. Taylor also released a solo album, *Feelings Are Good And Other Lies*.

It was a period of personal change for Taylor as well. In addition to having become sober, the bassist had gone through a divorce and then met his future wife, Juicy Couture designer Gela Nash. By early 1997, Taylor decided to leave Duran Duran altogether, announcing the news at a fan convention. As Rhodes told *Classic Pop Magazine* in 2023:

> John wanted to get his life together in California. He needed to make that decision. I resisted as much as I thought was sensible, but clearly, John's decision had been made. But it felt very strange having Warren, Simon and me.

Taylor went on to pursue his solo career and acting roles, appearing in several films, including ***Sugar Town*** and ***The Flintstones In Viva Rock Vegas***.

Duran Duran, now a threesome, forged ahead with their new album. However, in the wake of Taylor's departure, Le Bon had lost a key ally. During the recording of *Thank You*, two camps had reportedly emerged within the band: Le Bon and Taylor, and Rhodes and Cuccurullo, who also formed a production team/side project called TV Mania. Now more on his own within the band dynamic, the singer went on to pursue his own endeavour, Syn Productions, co-owned with his wife, Yasmin, and his friend Nick Woods. On *Medazzaland*, Le Bon shares a production credit with TV Mania under the Syn Pro Tokyo banner. Anthony J. Resta and Bob St. John, who contributed mixing that was at times heavy-handed on *Thank You*, are also credited as producers on several tracks.

Although the music on the album is inventive and enjoyable, its cover, by artist Andrew Day, is a bit chaotic. It features defaced images of the band members and phrases including 'Get over it' and 'Trans-Fat' scrawled across it. The title is stamped in the centre in shocking pink, and in the bottom right-hand corner, 'Duran Duran' appears as if scratched out in white lettering. The back cover has a drawing of the *Rio* cover model, disturbingly defaced in a similar fashion.

It was a chaotic time for the band, too. During the recording sessions for *Medazzaland*, Le Bon experienced significant writer's block, and Rhodes stepped in to write lyrics for several of the songs. During a time when Britpop was at its height, the band members sported that genre's shaggy hair but still dressed in colourful, shiny suits, and Rhodes wore just as much make-up as usual.

Even though the band, with only three members on board, explored modern electronic sounds on the album, it still sounded decidedly like Duran Duran, in large part due to Le Bon's distinctive vocals. Rhodes used analogue synths to give the music a warmth that some cutting-edge electronica lacked. The band also reached into the past, with references to their namesake, *Barbarella*, as well as Le Bon's close friend, Michael Hutchence of INXS.

When the final product was ready in late 1997, it landed with a thump in the US. In the UK, it wasn't released until 2021. The LP resurfaced on its 25th anniversary when it was reissued on CD and vinyl. Now that the album is widely available, perhaps it will gain the larger audience it has always deserved.

'Medazzaland' (Rhodes, Cuccurullo, Le Bon, Taylor)
The opening track has a throbbing bassline by Taylor, powerful drumming from Steve Alexander (who, along with bassist Wes Wehmiller, toured with the band at the time) and a rare turn as a lyricist and vocalist by Rhodes. The words, though written by the keyboardist, were reportedly inspired by Le Bon's writer's block and a trip to the dentist during which he was given the drug midazolam. 'I have no words left in me', Rhodes says in his droning, spoken-word vocals. He goes on to paint a picture of confusion. 'What are they saying about me?' he asks. 'Do they really understand what's wrong?'

The lyrics and eerie synths, in addition to 'vocal effects' by Cuccurullo's adopted son, Mayko, serve to set the mood for the album, informing the listener that they're about to 'sink deeper and deeper into Medazzaland'. The track was the opening song during their 1997 tour, and Rhodes admits that he's fond of it. He told *Stereogum* in 2015:

> I love 'Medazzaland' because it's a very unusual piece of music. It's much more experimental than a lot of the things we do. It was fun, actually, doing the vocal. I'm glad I didn't have to sing. It is very much spoken. But it was fun doing it live, actually. We used to open the show with it ... I could never remember all the words, so I put them inside a newspaper and read them.

'Big Bang Generation' (Rhodes, Cuccurullo, Le Bon, Taylor)
Cuccurullo's grinding guitar riff and Rhodes' synthesised bleeps drive this track, the second of four on the LP to feature Taylor. Le Bon delivers Rhodes' lyrics about an alien 'staring through a hole in the ozone', inspired by the keyboardist's belief that other life forms exist in the universe. Le Bon is joined by backup singer Sally Stapleton on the bridge leading into the outro, singing, 'When we gonna burn out? Don't know'. Noise guitar from Cuccurullo closes out the anthemic track.

'Electric Barbarella' (Rhodes, Cuccurullo, Le Bon)
Released as a single in September 1997. Chart places: US: 52, UK: 23
The album's second release was the first single by a major label act to be available to purchase for download online. The track, a standout on the album, is also noteworthy for its complex guitar work, a drum fill by Clem Burke of Blondie and clever lyrics. 'Emotionless and cold as ice', Le Bon intones dryly. 'All of the things I like'.

The song features an innovative solo from Cuccurullo followed by the sound of Rhodes' theremin-like synthesiser. (He used a Roland D-Beam during live performances of the track.) Once again, Le Bon shines on the anthemic chorus, singing, 'I plug you in. Dim the lights. Electric Barbarella'.

In the controversial video, directed by Ellen von Unwerth, the band members buy a robotic sex doll on Le Bon's credit card, unbox her and unleash her into the world. While their plan for the doll involves domestic duties like cleaning the house, as well as working as a waitress at a nightclub, she runs low on batteries and goes berserk. In the electronic press kit for the album, Le Bon describes the clip as 'definitely the most politically incorrect video we've made since 'Girls On Film'.' It was essentially censored, as it required additional edits for music television, all to receive only meagre airplay.

The single was unreleased in the UK until January 1999, when it was included on the *Greatest* album and charted higher than it initially had in the US.

'Out Of My Mind' (Rhodes, Cuccurullo, Le Bon)
Released as a single in March 1997. Chart place: UK: 21
The album's first single was featured on the soundtrack of the film *The Saint*. It features tabla and santoor by Talvin Singh, which, along with Dave DiCenso's drumming, gives the song an exotic feel. Layers of analogue and digital synths – including sound effects from Rhodes' Roland System-100 and strings from the Korg Trinity – wash over the haunting ballad, the third in a trilogy inspired by the memory of Le Bon's late friend David Miles. 'Light a candle. Lay flowers at the door', Le Bon sings at the deeper end of his register. 'For those who were left behind and the ones who've gone before'. In the bridge, he speaks in a near-whisper, 'How could you dare to become so real. When you're just a ghost in me'.

The gothic-style video, directed by Dean Karr, was filmed in Český Krumlov Castle in the Czech Republic. The visually striking clip depicts the band members as ghosts who haunt the castle's hallways. Le Bon also plays an old man – apparently inspired by the thatcher on the cover of *Led Zeppelin IV* – and, at one point, black liquid oozes from Cuccurullo's ear. Rhodes appears dressed in drag, wearing a Victorian-era dress and wig, and later opens a box to reveal a demon-like woman, whom he passionately kisses. It's among the band's most pretentious and over-the-top videos.

'Who Do You Think You Are?' (Rhodes, Cuccurullo, Le Bon)
This song's powerful lyrics have been interpreted as being about Taylor. But rather angry lines like 'your domination's through' and 'always trying to control me' don't seem to be about the bassist, who apparently was Le Bon's ally during the recording of *Thank You* and who also inspired another song on *Medazzaland* in which he's called a 'dear friend'. In the electronic press kit for the album, Le Bon sits beside Cuccurullo. 'It's a real anthem', the singer says. 'It had to have a really true sentiment for the lyric. And finally, I found one.' Indeed, the song is about his strained relationship with Cuccurullo, the singer revealed in a retrospective to mark the 20th anniversary of the album.

The idea for the track stemmed from plans to write a Christmas song but ended up in a very different place. The music – including powerful guitar riffs and a mix of analogue and digital synths – initially has a festive feel but turns into a showcase for Le Bon to vent his emotions. 'Sometimes I play along, but man I've got a mind!' he sings. At the end, he delivers his final cutting lines: 'It's just occurred to me. A possibility. The thought that you might really want to be me'.

'Silva Halo' (Rhodes, Cuccurullo, Le Bon)
This short track is instrumentally innovative but lyrically thin. It's essentially a poem by Rhodes that ends with Le Bon singing, 'Come to heaven silva halo'. The song sets the mood for the track about obsession that follows, as well as the standout ballads, which fill most of the remainder of the album. The song was played at the start of some of the band's live shows during the period.

'Be My Icon' (Rhodes, Cuccurullo, Le Bon)
This song about obsession features synthesised beeps and hard rock guitar riffs. 'I love you so much I keep your cigarette butts', Le Bon sings in the guise of a stalker. 'I built you a shrine. Now you can be my icon'.

The track features Taylor on bass, though he doesn't have a writing credit on it. Layers of synths and delayed guitars lend an uneasy edge to the song, and Le Bon's vocal performance is one of his best on the album.

Cuccurullo's innovative work on the LP was due in part to his rack, built around two Lexicon JamMans (audio looping devices), complemented by a range of rackmount effects and pedals. His first, called Delilah, was built in 1986, the guitarist told *Keyboard* magazine in 1998. 'Delilah was like a one-man band concept. I could do all kinds of looping and then just control things with my feet. I play just as much with my feet as I do with my hands.'

'Buried In The Sand' (Rhodes, Cuccurullo, Le Bon)
Rhodes wrote this song's lyrics about Taylor and his departure from the band. Le Bon's whispered introduction is followed by a sarangi sample that gives the track an Eastern vibe. 'I'm glad that you came along. But here our journey ends. I say goodbye to you', he sings in reference to Taylor. 'My very dear friend'. Synth bass and layers of additional synths form the outro to the song, which is the first in a series of three deeply personal tracks.

'Michael You've Got A Lot To Answer For' (Rhodes, Cuccurullo, Le Bon)
Le Bon's tribute to Hutchence and their friendship includes some of the album's best lyrics. In the mid-1990s, the INXS singer fuelled a tabloid media firestorm in the UK when he became romantically involved with Paula Yates, a British television presenter and Bob Geldof's then-wife. A custody battle between Geldof and Yates ensued. 'Trust you to get caught up in somebody's war', Le

Bon sings, adding hopefully, 'You'll come out of it all in time, I'm sure'. The song draws to a close with his plaintive words: 'And I know you're gonna call. If you need me. When you need me'. Less than two months after the release of *Medazzaland*, Hutchence was found dead in his hotel room in Sydney.

Cuccurullo's acoustic guitar, Rhodes' gentle synths and a touch of saxophone add tenderness to the track. It closes with strummed guitar chords that further evoke a sorrowful mood.

'Midnight Sun' (Rhodes, Cuccurullo, Le Bon, Taylor)
This ballad, perhaps the album's best track, features layers of synths and guitars, as well as live cello and a great bassline. (Taylor helped write the song but isn't credited with playing on it.) Le Bon references lyrics from 'Falling Angel', one of the band's best B-sides, with 'I'm dangling up in the blue', but adds a whimsical touch with 'And it's a cartoon coyote eternity before I drop down to you'. Cuccurullo plays an inspired riff before Le Bon asks, 'What am I supposed to do now?' A bass flourish is added towards the end of the song as Le Bon sings, 'You and I don't always fly. Let me go I want to fall'. The singer has only said that the wistful song is about someone special.

'So Long Suicide' (Rhodes, Cuccurullo, Le Bon)
On this track, which features Taylor, Le Bon addresses Kurt Cobain's suicide in 1994. It starts quietly in the verse before launching into a full-on glam rock chorus. 'Hello, I'm alive', Le Bon sings. 'In my bones, I know what I'm doing'.

While Duran Duran's musical style was quite different from Nirvana's, the grunge band had covered 'Rio' live. In addition, Cobain's wife, Courtney Love, played 'Hungry Like The Wolf' with her band Hole on *MTV Unplugged*. So, it wouldn't be far-fetched to say that the couple had at least some appreciation for Duran Duran, who, in turn, felt the impact of Cobain's music and untimely death. Although Le Bon couldn't contemplate suicide himself, he still had empathy for Cobain. As Le Bon told *Keyboard* magazine in 1998:

> I just thought he was such a brilliant musician. It's like van Gogh dying. It really hurt me a lot, and it stayed with me a long time. I just wanted to write a song that would say that I can say goodbye now. 'Cause I've got to live, I'm not like that. Suicide's not going to be the end of my life.

'Undergoing Treatment' (Rhodes, Cuccurullo, Le Bon)
This Beatles-esque track includes cheeky lyrics, acoustic guitar and a vaguely hip-hop beat, which together make for an unconventional album closer. Le Bon channels John Lennon as he sings, 'If you see me walking in the garden, don't ever ask me for an autograph'. Strings build throughout the bridge, leading into a whistled melody that draws further comparisons to the Fab Four.

Rhodes has said that the 'madcap song' is about the band and their treatment by the music industry. The track includes references to the mid-price section and *Q* magazine before ending with the sound of a door slamming shut – presumably on a band many would have preferred to 'disappear like dinosaurs' – closing the album in a brilliant fashion.

Extra Tracks

'Ball And Chain' (Rhodes, Cuccurullo, Le Bon, Taylor)
This bonus track on the Japanese edition of the album, with its hard-edged guitars and processed vocals, is a departure for Duran Duran. The song is also notable for its heavy rhythm section and glam-infused lyrics, which reference a subject who is 'street gutter crawling when the sun comes up'. While the song was perhaps too experimental to have made the album, it was released digitally as a single, along with a lyric video to mark the 25th anniversary of *Medazzaland* in 2022.

'Sinner Or Saint' (Rhodes, Cuccurullo, Le Bon, Taylor)
This track, a B-side on versions of both the album's singles, is a straight-up rock song about watching 'humankind stumble into another century'. The guitar-driven track opens with a killer riff from Cuccurullo and features mostly understated synths, as well as 'fuzz bass' from Taylor. Le Bon delivers the spoken-word lines – 'Some people love too fast. Some people live too long. And so I've got to ask. Do you know right from wrong?' – with each line punctuated by a guitar riff before he again reaches into a higher register. The song, which was submitted for *The Saint* soundtrack but passed over in favour of 'Out Of My Mind', is still a standout B-side.

As the new century approached, Duran Duran were once again feeling their way forward. It was uncertain whether they could find success again as a diminished band with only two original members amid an ever-changing music scene. However, as always, they were determined to persevere.

Pop Trash (2000)

Personnel:
Simon Le Bon: vocals
Nick Rhodes: keyboards
Warren Cuccurullo: guitars, bass
Additional musicians:
David Campbell: string arrangements
Mark Tinley: programming
John Tonks: drums, electronic percussion
Steve Alexander: drums
Gregg Bissonette: drums
Luis Conte: percussion
Sally Boyden: vocals
Guy Farley: acoustic piano
Recorded at Privacy from 1999 to 2000
Produced by TV Mania in association with Syn Productions
Engineers: Mark Tinley and Ken Scott
Record label: Hollywood Records
Release date: June 2000
Highest chart places: UK: 53, US: 135
Running time: 59:10
Current edition: 2022 BMG CD/2023 BMG LP

As the year 2000 approached, Duran Duran were still Taylor-less and without a record company after parting ways with EMI/Capitol. However, there was something happening in pop culture that could only be favourable for the band. In the late 1990s, there was a 1980s revival that kept growing into the 2000s and beyond. Duran Duran capitalised, though not with their new music.

Nevertheless, they were commonly cited as an influence on a variety of musical acts. In the late 1990s, there were two Duran Duran tribute albums released: one by young punk bands like Deftones and Jimmy Eat World and the other by Australian artists, including Kylie Minogue. In 1998, the band dropped a second, more extensive album of their greatest hits, simply and boldly titled *Greatest*, and soon scored their latest platinum album.

They were also still a formidable force as a live act, boosted by Cuccurullo's powerful playing and their new rhythm section of Wes Wehmiller and Joe Travers, both brought on board by the guitarist. The band often took chances in their live shows, regularly changing their setlists and often arranging songs in innovative ways. With sales of their new records at a low point, they relied increasingly on touring mostly small to mid-size venues.

The band, driven as always to keep recording new material, forged ahead with plans for a new album. They played some of those songs live before signing a new record deal, this time with Disney-owned Hollywood Records.

Le Bon again experienced writer's block, so Rhodes contributed lyrics and Cuccurullo wrote melodies for many of the songs. At the urging of their engineer Ken Scott – who had worked with The Beatles, Bowie and Cuccurullo's own Missing Persons – the band used vintage guitars and amps, as well as analogue synths, including the Jupiter-8, with the goal of achieving a more organic sound. Though a version of the LP mixed by Scott was finished, ultimately, the band opted to remix the album before its release to make it sound more modern.

The album cover, designed by Andrew Day, features a photo of Liberace's rhinestone-encrusted Mercedes Excalibur and 'Pop Trash' in silver lettering with the band's name underneath. The images inside reference other pop culture kitsch, including a model dressed in lingerie holding a machine gun and the band members wearing clothing like silver leather pants and animal-print shirts.

Although Duran Duran continued to be a successful touring act, their new album again failed to ignite the charts, and Le Bon became increasingly disenchanted with the situation. 'I felt very strongly that somebody had pulled the plug from the bath and let the water drain away', he told *Entertainment Weekly* in 2004. 'I'd had it with the [2000] lineup and I wasn't going to do it anymore.'

Pop Trash yielded only one single, 'Someone Else Not Me', and both the band's new record deal and the Rhodes/Le Bon/Cuccurullo lineup turned out to be short-lived, but there was still time to revive Duran Duran and their legacy. As John Taylor told *Vulture* in 2002:

> The gem that I think went by was 'Someone Else Not Me' from *Pop Trash*. It's up there with 'Ordinary World' for me. It's an absolute beauty, but it was just one of those times. It really didn't matter. I mean, I wasn't a part of the band then, and people were looking in another direction with Duran Duran. If you have a long career, you're going to have times when nobody cares ... [But] at some point, people are going to come back around, reconsider you and put you in the Rock & Roll Hall of Fame.

'Someone Else Not Me' (Rhodes, Le Bon, Cuccurullo)
Released as a single in March 2000. Chart place: UK: 53
The album's first and only single in the UK and the US features lyrics by Le Bon and a descending guitar riff from Cuccurullo reminiscent of 'Come Undone'. The song was an attempt at success on the scale of that single and 'Ordinary World', but charted only in the UK. The ballad boasts classic rock-style guitar and lush strings; Rhodes used both Akai S3200 and Kurzweil K2000 synths for much of the strings and piano on the album. But the track, with its slower tempo, ultimately didn't fit into a music scene then dominated by boy bands and other pop acts.

The video, created by Fullerene Productions, employed Flash animation, then a groundbreaking innovation that Duran Duran were the first to use in a music video. Fullerene went on to create videos for Beck's 'Nicotine & Gravy' and Queens of the Stone Age's 'Feel Good Hit Of The Summer' – both cutting-edge artists at the time. Duran Duran's clip features images of the band in black-and-white amid colourful graphics that bring to mind The Beatles' *Yellow Submarine*.

Versions of the song were also released in French and Spanish.

'Lava Lamp' (Rhodes, Le Bon, Cuccurullo)
This upbeat track with poppy lyrics, quirky synths, catchy guitar and an Eastern flair could have been a candidate for a feel-good summer single. The band perhaps highlighted the song's potential by naming their *Let It Flow* tour after one of its lines.

Le Bon addresses a woman with a 'many coloured halo. The body of Venus, a babe rainbow', and the equally light, sexually suggestive chorus consists solely of 'La-la-la-la lava lamp. I'd love to turn you on'. The song proves that, sometimes, simple can be good, especially when it comes to pop music.

'Playing With Uranium' (Rhodes, Le Bon, Cuccurullo)
Duran Duran explore their rock-oriented side on this track, for which Rhodes wrote lyrics that were later tweaked by Le Bon. It was released as a single in Italy.

The song opens with Cuccurullo's creative riff and takes off with its anthemic chorus. 'Reinvent the human race', Le Bon sings. 'You just got the invitation'. The lyrics are, quite literally, about a person playing with uranium, inspired by a news story about a teenager who tried to build a nuclear reactor in a backyard shed. However, this could also easily be about the fortunes of the band: 'We go undiscovered 'cause people are careless', he sings. 'One way or another, they'll never forget us'.

'Hallucinating Elvis' (Rhodes, Le Bon, Cuccurullo)
The album's only real dud features Rhodes' lyrics that reference Elvis Presley, some great guitar work from Cuccurullo and Le Bon's awkward vocal style that borders on rapping.

Rhodes has said that the song is about a person on a flight from 'Hawaii to Las Vegas' who believes they're turning into Presley himself. 'FBI tapping the King's phone. '74, he's trapped in his home', Le Bon speaks in the bridge. The track is brought down by the spoken-word vocals as well as its repetitive chorus, which consists mostly of the words in the title; it probably could have benefited from the singer's input.

'Starting To Remember' (Rhodes, Le Bon, Cuccurullo)
With this Beatles-esque ballad, the album gets back on track and doesn't let the listener down from there. Rhodes' basic but lovely lyrics reference Pablo Picasso – 'Draw like a child' – and Le Bon sings them in a smooth tenor. Amid

Guy Farley's acoustic piano and Cuccurullo's acoustic guitar, Le Bon delivers wistful lines about rediscovering joy in life: 'I was happy ever after. Was it only yesterday that I bought the dream?'

'Pop Trash Movie' (Rhodes, Cuccurullo)
During the lead-up to *Pop Trash*, Rhodes and Cuccurullo wrote and produced two songs for the newly reunited Blondie. Although Blondie recorded a version of 'Pop Trash Movie', it was never officially released. (The other track, 'Studio 54', had a similar fate.) But Le Bon gladly sang the song, which even provided the title for the album. Arguably, he delivers it better than the singer for whom it was originally written.

Rhodes' lyrics reference his late friend Andy Warhol and the rumination about fame often attributed to the artist: 'We'll all be famous for 15 minutes'. In the stunning bridge, Le Bon sings emotively, 'I'll wait in the wings for you. I'll read your lines to you. But now the script is final. You know it's time to go'. Strings and the anthemic chorus follow, to which Le Bon dramatically whispers, 'Never', as the song nears its end. Cuccurullo adds an epic guitar solo before the music fades out.

'Fragment' (Rhodes, Le Bon, Cuccurullo)
This instrumental interlude serves merely as a bridge between a ballad and an up-tempo track. The band also created several similar brief instrumentals, titled 'Prototypes', which were included on some versions of the album as bonus tracks.

'Mars Meets Venus' (Rhodes, Le Bon, Cuccurullo)
This catchy track, with lyrics by Rhodes, is another album highlight. The keyboardist has stated that he was inspired by The Beatles' 'Being For The Benefit Of Mr. Kite!' – which was, in turn, inspired by a 19th-century circus poster bearing most of the words that would become that song's lyrics. Instead of a vintage poster, Rhodes took his cue from personal ads, and both songs are whimsical artistic statements.

As Le Bon lists descriptions of people looking for love, he could easily have veered into hip-hop territory but thankfully doesn't. 'Hippie chick for soul brother bluesman', he sings. 'Genuine American frog meets princess'. In the chorus, Le Bon sings, 'Someone is perfect for you', to which backup singer Sally Boyden adds, 'When Mars meets Venus'. Cuccurullo's guitar riffs and Rhodes' synths punctuate the song, leading into the outro, as Le Bon repeatedly sings, 'Here's looking at you'.

'Lady Xanax' (Rhodes, Le Bon, Cuccurullo)
The album offers up another standout ballad with the haunting 'Lady Xanax', featuring Rhodes' lyrics about a person who's become reliant on pharmaceuticals. In the verse, Le Bon sings in an almost dreamlike state – 'So

you paint with your mascara. Social eyes, don't look twice' – accompanied by Cuccurullo on acoustic guitar. In the chorus, he sings at the lower end of his register – 'Don't be afraid, afraid of what is on your mind' – punctuated by heavier guitar riffs. Rhodes completes the mood with the addition of strings and spacey synths.

'The Sun Doesn't Shine Forever' (Rhodes, Le Bon, Cuccurullo)
This straightforward ballad – a departure for Duran Duran – features standout guitar, lovely strings and tender lyrics that make for a pleasant listen. Le Bon sings of a failing relationship: 'At the end of the rainbow. Found each other there. Strange, we never thought the colours would fade'.

As evidenced on this track, Cuccurullo, who often plays in a more experimental manner, is also a virtuoso when it comes to more conventional musical styles. His solo ends the song and leads into the epic album closer, which also serves as a final showcase for the guitarist's work as a member of Duran Duran.

'Kiss Goodbye'/'Last Day On Earth' (Rhodes, Le Bon, Cuccurullo)
Though these two songs are listed as separate tracks, 'Kiss Goodbye' is essentially a brief instrumental that leads into 'Last Day On Earth'. Rhodes and Cuccurullo submitted an early version of the latter song to be considered for use in the Bond film *Tomorrow Never Dies*. It was passed over in favour of Sheryl Crow's effort, most likely because Duran Duran weren't considered a popular musical act at the time. 'Last Day On Earth' was released as a single in Japan.

However, the track, in which Le Bon asks, 'Now what would you do if there was no tomorrow?', would have been a fantastic theme song for a film called *Tomorrow Never Dies*. The outro consists of a bucket list of desires – 'Hoping, dreaming, smiling, laughing' and so on – before Le Bon emotively adds, 'Your last day on Earth'. Then, the music fades out, closing the door on another era of Duran Duran.

Astronaut (2004)

Personnel:
Simon Le Bon: vocals
Nick Rhodes: keyboards
Andy Taylor: guitars, vocals
John Taylor: bass
Roger Taylor: drums
Additional musicians:
Mark Tinley: programming
Lily Gonzalez: percussion
Guy Farley: string arrangements
Sally Boyden: vocals
Tessa Niles: vocals
Jason Nevins: programming
Recorded at Sphere Studios from 2001 to 2004
Produced by Duran Duran, Don Gilmore, Dallas Austin and Nile Rodgers
Engineers: Don Gilmore, Dallas Austin, Mark Tinley
Record label: Epic Records
Release date: October 2004
Highest chart places: UK: 3, US: 17
Running time: 49:52
Current edition: 2022 BMG CD/LP

The seeds of an exciting development were starting to bear fruit in the new decade. Eighties nostalgia was growing, culminating with the rise of bands that wouldn't exist if not for Duran Duran and their new wave peers. This list included The Killers, Franz Ferdinand, Interpol and Scissor Sisters. No Doubt and other mainstream acts also joined them on the 1980s bandwagon. The Strokes – whose guitarist Nick Valensi wore a *Rio* shirt and even married John Taylor's ex-wife, Amanda de Cadenet – were in some ways a grittier Fab Five for the 2000s. It seemed as if a Duran Duran reunion couldn't have been far behind.

Indeed, as far back as 1999, Le Bon and Taylor had reunited onstage at Joe's Pub in Manhattan, performing 'Rio' and The Power Station's 'Some Like It Hot'. All the while, the classic lineup remained in talks to get back together and eventually announced the big news in 2001.

Cuccurullo was asked to leave the band so that the original members could get back together. According to the guitarist, a deal was worked out in which he would be compensated for the forthcoming album from the reunited band. Cuccurullo – who in 2001 had posed nude in *G Magazine*, a Brazilian publication – went on to briefly reform Missing Persons, make further forays into adult entertainment with a website and the release of the 'Rock Rod' and eventually open a restaurant.

In the meantime, Rhodes stayed busy with two notable side projects. He reunited with original Duran Duran vocalist Stephen Duffy for The Devils.

The duo revived some of the band's material from their earliest days for their excellent album, *Dark Circles*. Rhodes also produced an LP for American band The Dandy Warhols, *Welcome To The Monkey House*, which was released in 2003 and to which Le Bon contributed back-up vocals. The album featured the Duran Duran pastiche 'You Were The Last High' – which was released as a single, complete with a video that paid tribute to 'Planet Earth'.

While Duran Duran were steadily gaining cultural cachet – and there was palpable excitement among their existing fan base for their reunion – the recording industry remained cool to the idea. The band had decided not to cash in with live shows but to begin recording a new album instead. However, without a record deal, the members had to self-finance some of the sessions.

To drum up public interest in the reunion – and amass some much-needed cash – the band finally announced a Japanese tour in 2003. The shows sold out quickly, and successful tours of the US and the UK followed. In the US, they played their first reunion show at The Roxy Theatre in West Hollywood, California, in July 2003. The concert was attended by some of the biggest names in popular music – including Beck, No Doubt's Gwen Stefani (a rumoured guest artist on the new album) and Bush's Gavin Rossdale. In the UK, the band played larger venues and brought along two present-day groups as opening acts: Scissor Sisters and Goldfrapp.

It was nothing short of exhilarating to see the Fab Five back together live for the first time in nearly two decades. There was a new energy during the initial reunion shows, which featured only the original members and no additional musicians. (Andy and John Taylor ably sang backup.) The back-to-basics approach was refreshing, and the band soaked in the audience's adoration as the members stood in silhouette at the front of the stage each night.

After the band started focusing on their live shows – at the urging of their manager, Wendy Laister, who had formerly managed Aerosmith – the industry was finally beginning to take notice. Duran Duran picked up two lifetime achievement awards, from MTV and *Q*, the latter of which was particularly noteworthy because the magazine's critics had lambasted their music in the not-too-distant past. They were also honoured with an Outstanding Contribution to Music award at The Brits. In June 2004, they inked a recording deal, signing with Epic Records.

From the very first meeting of the newly reunited band, Rhodes and Andy Taylor, who had been at odds at times over the band's direction in the past, were both set on recording a new album. But that was about the only matter they agreed upon, Taylor wrote in his autobiography, *Wild Boy*. In his book, the guitarist also expressed unease over Rhodes' and Le Bon's insistence that he and Roger Taylor receive a smaller percentage of the band's earnings and detailed disagreements over lyrics, which Le Bon delivered despite again experiencing writer's block. However, the band forged ahead and eventually turned in a new album nearly three years after the reunion was officially announced.

Le Bon recounted in the electronic press kit for *Astronaut* that, despite any disagreements, the members could always eventually find common ground. 'Roger and I are more kind of central and more in the middle of it all,' he said, 'and we often find that we're the glue that holds the band together. We're always the ones who pull the extremes together.'

Astronaut was recorded, in part, in the south of France and at Sphere Studios in London with assistance from Linkin Park producer Don Gilmore, r&b hitmaker Dallas Austin and the band's old friend Nile Rodgers. The varied backgrounds of the co-producers and the musical preferences of the band members themselves – including the traditional guitar rock that Andy Taylor had pursued during his solo career and the electronic dance music beloved by Roger Taylor – were reflected on the final album. Yet, in the end, *Astronaut* was a bit of a mixed bag, which included attempts at a modern-day chart-topper but also sought to please the most die-hard Duranies – and fell a bit short on both counts.

The album cover features a moody black-and-white photo of the band members by Kristian Schuller against a white background with pink brushstroke-like flourishes. In the inside band photo by Richard Haughton, the members strike a Roxy Music pose, each one holding a guitar in a re-creation of the famous image from the *For Your Pleasure* LP.

Astronaut was a success in the UK, yielding a top-five hit and achieving gold status there. Overall, the album was a pleasant listen, which served as a reminder of what Duran Duran still could achieve. It took a few years for the band members to find their footing and their place amid the current musical landscape, but their reunion album was an important first step for a revived band who ultimately hoped to cement their legacy.

'(Reach Up For The) Sunrise' (Duran Duran)

Released as a single in August 2004. Chart places: UK: 5, US: 89

The Fab Five's comeback single is an uplifting track that charted well in the UK and in many countries around the world. Its most famous iteration – and the one the band most often perform live – is the dancefloor-friendly remix by Jason Nevins, which was included on the soundtrack to the popular television show *Queer Eye For The Straight Guy*.

Le Bon has described the track as 'pure frivolity' and 'essential Duran Duran'. It's among a batch of joyous songs on an album that also includes more sombre fare. Indeed, several upbeat tracks were written in the south of France before the 11 September attacks on the US, which in turn influenced the moodier material to come. Synths, including an organ-like keyboard riff throughout, are front and centre on the song, which also has a soaring chorus, a catchy bassline and dynamic drumming. But as on much of the lineup's last studio album, *Seven And The Ragged Tiger*, the guitars seem to be buried in the mix on 'Sunrise'.

The video, directed by The Polish Brothers (Michael and Mark Polish), follows each member in his own storyline and shows the band performing together in front of a brilliant sunrise. Le Bon rides a motorcycle, John Taylor walks through a desert carrying a guitar case and Rhodes appears to pilot a spaceship, communicating with his doppelgänger on a city street below via flashlight. Roger Taylor is shown in a bedroom and driving a car, while Andy Taylor walks on a beach and visits a nightclub.

While 'Sunrise' wasn't the huge hit the band hoped for, it remains an enduring anthem that still occasionally appears in their live setlists.

'Want You More!' (Duran Duran)
This up-tempo track, co-produced by Austin, features more abundant guitar but also plenty of keyboards. On much of the album, Rhodes used his Roland V-Synth – a synthesiser with both analogue and digital inputs – to shape the sound. Le Bon adds energetic vocals and straightforward lyrics that touch on manipulation and desire. The track features modern flourishes, including a cool vocal effect as he sings, 'Drivin' the car. Turn up the sound' – the track does sound great cranked up during a drive. Like 'Sunrise', it's frivolous, fun and sounds like vintage Duran Duran, but updated for the 2000s.

'What Happens Tomorrow' (Duran Duran)
Released as a single in January 2005. Chart place: UK: 11
The album's second single nearly hit the top ten in the UK and is one of the LP's best tracks. It was even better in its earlier, live version, which included a bridge later used for the B-side 'Silent Icy River'. The song features Le Bon's tender lyrics and trademark harmonies, as well as the album's first real guitar solo. 'Fighting because we're so close. There are times we punish those who we need the most', Le Bon sings in a line that could be about the state of the world or Duran Duran themselves. Rhodes adds synthesised strings, and the rhythm section ably round out the track. As in the band's early days, Andy Taylor's guitar adds a bit of edginess, which gives the song a classic rock feel.

In the video, directed by Smith n' Borin (Ryan Smith and Frank Buff Borin), the band members appear as constellations in the night sky as a couple watch their performance from the hood of a car. While the young couple are dressed casually, the members look like dapper gents in their dark suits.

The song is one of Duran Duran's most overlooked singles and deserved to be a far bigger hit.

'Astronaut' (Duran Duran)
The LP's title track, also co-produced by Austin, begins quietly with acoustic guitar and builds from there, eventually culminating in layers of swirling synths and becoming hampered by an everything-and-the-kitchen-sink production style. With a range of collaborators and the use of Pro Tools software, the *Astronaut* album is widely considered to be overproduced.

However, even this track shows that Duran Duran benefit by embracing simplicity, as in the bridge, in which John Taylor's bass is allowed to stand out and Le Bon sings dreamily, 'Bare-feet for quantum leap, because space is hot and deep. And we follow giant footprints as we fall'. Yet, ultimately, there's just too much going on in the song for it to be a successful effort.

'Bedroom Toys' (Duran Duran)
Funky bass and guitar, as well as pleasant backup vocals from frequent collaborator Tessa Niles, can't save this track, the album's only true dud. The lyrics – about sex toys and 'pimps and snitches to dip into your riches' – are further hampered by Le Bon's vocals, which border on rapping as he repeats the line 'Oh my God what's this?' The track may have been intended to be cheeky, but it comes off as cringeworthy and just doesn't fit the style of the rest of the album.

'Nice' (Duran Duran)
The album gets back on track with one of its best songs. Le Bon's outstanding vocals build in the chorus with the simple lines: 'There is nothing better than being with you. And I'm feeling so nice'. The song succeeds because all the band members are given a chance to shine. John Taylor delivers a throbbing bassline, Andy Taylor plays some well-timed guitar licks, Roger Taylor lends the track a driving beat and Rhodes adds some of his signature synth work.

The song was released digitally in 2005 – along with remixes of the track – and as a promotional single in Europe. Though it failed to gain traction with listeners well after the album's release, it may have fared better than 'What Happens Tomorrow' as the LP's second single.

'Taste The Summer' (Duran Duran)
This infectious song features disco-inflected bass and guitar, layers of synths and subtly processed backup vocals. Le Bon begins the track with the repeated line 'do-do-do, do-be-do' before delivering rather simple lyrics that scream summertime at every turn. 'Wild orchid on the wind you know just where it's blowing', he sings. 'So fresh; from your lips is born the melody'. The outro is a bit repetitive but doesn't drag down the song, which is yet another feel-good moment on an album brimming with them.

'Finest Hour' (Duran Duran)
This ballad, whose title references Prime Minister Winston Churchill's famous speech, has an anthemic chorus whose lyrics are a commentary about the state of the world after the 9/11 attacks. 'Been under quiet attack, but now it's time for you and me', Le Bon sings. 'If we're gonna take it back you've got to fight for what you believe'. His vocals are superb, Rhodes' synths seem to produce a 'breaking news' sound effect and Andy Taylor adds understated guitar riffs throughout the song.

'Finest Hour' is the first of several tracks showcasing Duran Duran's more serious side that are as good or better than the more light-hearted material that dominates the first half of the album.

'Chains' (Duran Duran)
This fine effort is driven by John Taylor's galloping bassline and Andy Taylor's jangly acoustic guitar. Le Bon, in a 2005 US television appearance on *Northwest Afternoon*, described the song as being about 'a guy who sits on his porch every night, and he feels the demons come to drag him off ... He has to fight them away so he can wake up the next day.'

Le Bon starts the song quietly before launching into a higher register in the chorus, singing, 'I put my hand into the flame. Burning but I feel no pain'. The words touch on other dark images, including 'ghosts' creeping in and 'dark shapes' gathering around. Following the bridge, which consists mainly of Le Bon singing 'Na, na, na, na, na, na' and Andy Taylor's electric guitar, the song builds into a bass- and synth-filled outro to close this hauntingly beautiful track.

'One Of Those Days' (Duran Duran)
The final song that was co-produced by Austin and the last finished for the album features soaring vocals and a Beatles-esque melody. A vocal sample counts in the track before Le Bon launches into the verse, on which he's accompanied by guitar. In the chorus, he sings defiantly, 'Seen better times than right now. But I'm not running away'. In the outro, the 'one, two' sample returns, joined by synthesised bleeps, both of which cause the otherwise solid song to peter out a bit at the end. Nevertheless, the track is a statement of hope amid a string of more subdued moments.

'Point Of No Return' (Duran Duran)
This album highlight was co-produced by Rodgers and has an almost hypnotic groove thanks to the Chic founder. Rhodes snaps his fingers to start the track and adds understated synths, and John and Roger Taylor lock in for a funky rhythm. The song, which is about 9/11, may be the band's most pointed political statement. As Rhodes told *Stereogum* in 2015:

> It's about the Twin Towers. Obviously, that had a profound effect on all of us at the time when it happened. It was very difficult to actually approach the subject with a song, but we felt the need to do it. I said one day, 'Well, we've reached the point of no return, haven't we?' It stuck as a song title.

'Naivety falls from our eyes', Le Bon sings. 'And we'll not regain. As we watch the tower falling down'. In the pre-chorus, he adds with resignation, 'Maybe things can change', before singing plaintively, 'You know there's no avoiding the lesson to be learned'. The track also features a bluesy guitar solo from

Andy Taylor. Duran Duran are at their best here, thanks in part to Rodgers, who clearly knows how to showcase their talents.

'Still Breathing' (Duran Duran)
This downtempo track has yet another great bassline and haunting lyrics that again bring to mind 9/11, which was still fresh in memory more than three years later. The song opens with layers of synths as Le Bon sings in a lower register until the second verse. 'Heart, though it's hot and quiet', he then adds emotively. 'My head is cool and quiet as the ashes that fall from the sky'. A 'sound collage' of synths, bass and drums closes the track to end the album on a sombre note.

The choice to end their reunion album with a song about survival, whether of humankind or just the band, couldn't be more perfect, especially in retrospect.

Extra Tracks
'Virus' (Duran Duran)
This song, a bonus track on the Japanese edition of the album, is the most rock-oriented effort from the *Astronaut* sessions. It's among many fine tracks that didn't make it onto the LP in other countries. In fact, the band wrote more than 30 songs, more than half of which were in the running for the album at one point. 'Virus' was also played live during their initial reunion concerts.

The track is about a topic of its time, a computer virus, and perhaps could have become dated in the years to follow. But it remains as relevant as ever as computers continue to become ever more dominant. 'When I interface ... Nothing will remain', Le Bon sings. 'Everything will change forever'. The song, with its driving bassline, incendiary guitar and understated synths, is one of the band's catchiest songs from the reunion era (pun not intended).

'Know It All' (Duran Duran)
This track, the B-side on the 'Sunrise' single, is a synth-driven track with minimal, heavily processed vocals. Along with 'Silent Icy River', it's a puzzling choice for a B-side, especially when the band had several other demos that were more fully formed as songs.

'Silent Icy River' (Duran Duran)
This B-side of 'What Happens Tomorrow' consists mainly of the bridge from an earlier iteration of that song. Its lyrics, including 'time is a ribbon, a silent icy river' and 'tiny lives mean everything', made an excellent bridge. But this track seems more like an unfinished piece of music.

'Beautiful Colours' (Duran Duran)
Although this song was never officially released, a polished demo exists. It was played at a FIFA Centennial event and performed by the band during

their initial reunion shows. (Other demos from the *Astronaut* era include 'Salt In The Rainbow', 'Pretty Ones', 'Lonely Business' and 'TV Vs. Radio'.)

However, this anthemic track has always deserved an official release and is more than worthy of covering here. In fact, it's one of the best songs from the reunion years and features some of the trademarks of the band's classic sound: a solid vocal and melody, uplifting lyrics and bubbly synths. With the mantra 'Live through this. Keep breathing. Keep loving', the song could have been a contender for a comeback single, but the band decided that there was room for improvement and, as with a plethora of their other material – and an entire album to come – it was left on the cutting-room floor.

Red Carpet Massacre (2007)

Personnel:
Simon Le Bon: vocals
Nick Rhodes: keyboards
John Taylor: bass
Roger Taylor: drums
Additional musicians:
Dom Brown: guitars
Timbaland: vocals
Justin Timberlake: vocals
Jim Beanz: vocals
Terri Walker: vocals
Simon Willescroft: saxophone
Recorded at Sphere Studios, The Manhattan Center, Metropolis Studios and Sarm Studios from 2006 to 2007
Produced by Nate 'Danja' Hills, Jimmy Douglass, Duran Duran, Timbaland and Justin Timberlake
Engineers: Jimmy Douglass, Marcella 'Ms. Lago' Araica, Matt Lawrence, Jean-Marie Horvat, Matthew Hager
Record label: Epic Records
Release date: November 2007
Highest chart places: UK: 44, US: 36
Running time: 48:52
Current edition: 2022 BMG CD/LP

Following the mildly successful *Astronaut* album, Duran Duran were back on tour, playing a mix of theatres and arenas in the US in the spring of 2005. However, for several of the shows, a fifth of the Fab Five was missing, as Andy Taylor had returned to the UK to cope with the illness of his father, who later died. Guitarist Dom Brown of Manchester entered the picture, filling Taylor's shoes temporarily and eventually permanently. Though Brown has never been named an official member, his stint with the band has been longer than either Taylor's or Cuccurullo's.

The story of Taylor's departure revolves partially around a familiar point of contention: the band's musical direction. The follow-up to *Astronaut* was intended to be an album called *Reportage*, which was reportedly rock-oriented and included protest songs against the Iraq War. It was produced by Michael Patterson, who worked with Beck on the excellent *Midnite Vultures* album, as well as with a range of other acts, including Black Rebel Motorcycle Club and The Notorious B.I.G. At one point, Duran Duran were also slated to work with producer Youth, the bassist of Killing Joke (of 'Eighties' fame) before scrapping the album altogether. The LP has remained under wraps since, though in recent years, the band members have discussed finally releasing it.

After receiving feedback about the new material from Epic that was less than enthusiastic, the band decided to switch gears entirely. At the urging of the record company, they would begin working with hip-hop star Timbaland and singer Justin Timberlake.

Although Taylor wasn't happy about this new direction, there were also technical and health reasons behind his departure from the band, which he detailed in his autobiography. In 2006, a problem with his US visa prevented him from attending the recording sessions with Timbaland, and depression lingering from the impact of his father's death kept him from performing that autumn. In October of that year, the band posted a statement on their website saying that 'there is an unworkable gulf between us and we can no longer effectively function together'.

The Fab Five's last song recorded together during the reunion era, which wasn't released until 2007, was a foot-stomping version of John Lennon's 'Instant Karma!' On their first and only recorded cover of a song by a Beatle, they added signature Le Bon harmonies and a trademark John Taylor bassline. The track, which appears on the compilation album ***Instant Karma: The Amnesty International Campaign To Save Darfur***, also harked back in the best way to their first released cover: Bowie's 'Fame'. For nearly two more decades, it stood as a fitting final recording with Andy Taylor.

Meanwhile, *Red Carpet Massacre*, the result of the sessions with Timbaland and Timberlake, was taking shape. Although Duran Duran had never been afraid to get funky, their past attempts at hip-hop had been frightful. Duranies rightfully had doubts that the band's DNA would be detected in the new endeavour. As Rhodes told *The Quietus* in 2011:

> We got an opportunity to work with Timbaland, so we thought, 'Great, let's go for it'. We knew it was a risk in terms of what the fans would like, especially if you're working with someone who is ostensibly an electro/hip-hop producer. When Timbaland saw the guitar, bass and drums come into the studio, I think he was *mortified* because everything's in a box for those guys.

Timberlake, who had risen to fame in the boy band NSYNC and was known for his harmonies with the vocal group, had professed his admiration for Duran Duran when he presented them with their lifetime achievement award at the Brits in 2004. But now he was a bona fide r&b star and part of an 'it' production team. The band worked with Timbaland and Timberlake on a few songs for the album in New York before returning to London for additional recording sessions with Timbaland protégé Nate 'Danja' Hills, who co-produced the majority of the album.

Timberlake made his biggest impact on the album with its first and only single, which leaned into one of the LP's recurring themes: celebrity culture. The singer had never been bigger after he mined his past relationship with pop star Britney Spears for his hit single 'Cry Me A River' – even going so far as to feature a look-alike actress in the music video. Yet, Spears was in a mental health spiral and had been vilified in the media for cheating on Timberlake when, in fact, he had also been unfaithful to her.

Duran Duran's 'Falling Down' – co-written and co-produced by Timberlake – is in some ways the spiritual successor to 'Cry Me A River'. Band members have said that the song was inspired by Spears' struggles, as well as those of other female celebrities, and a Spears look-alike was again cast in its video. Timberlake has since apologised to the singer for past actions and acknowledged that he 'benefitted from a system that condones misogyny', though he has since walked back that statement. Regardless, it's clear that in 2007 – and perhaps still today – the glare of celebrity shone brighter on female stars.

The theme of celebrity culture extends to the album's cover, which features a photo taken by Rhodes of a fallen starlet, scantily clad and surrounded by other models, one standing with a high heel over her chest – literally, a red-carpet massacre. Long-time collaborator Patty Palazzo completed the design, with art direction by John Taylor. The members have stated that the artwork is meant to be tongue-in-cheek.

To promote the album, the band took to Broadway, performing the LP in full as well as an inspired 'electro set' of some of their classic songs at the Ethel Barrymore Theatre and the Roseland Ballroom. Even though the Broadway stint served to stir up excitement among the band's fan base, their foray into urban music turned out to be short-lived. The album sold poorly in both the US and the UK and left them without a recording contract once again. However, its commercial performance was perhaps what Duran Duran – without their guitarist and seemingly without a direction – needed in order to find their way.

'The Valley' (Duran Duran, Hills)

The album's first track is a hopeful sign that Timbaland and Timberlake have perhaps left Duran Duran's musical integrity intact. But alas, 'The Valley' is one of the songs on the LP co-produced by Hills, who helped make the project salvageable. The producer has a writing credit on all songs from the *Red Carpet Massacre* sessions save for 'Falling Down'. Notably, he's the first co-producer to share songwriting credit with the band members – but not the last.

'The Valley' is a valiant effort. Along with songs like 'Box Full O' Honey' and 'She's Too Much', the track actually sounds like Duran Duran performing as a band and not Le Bon singing over Timbaland's beats. On the track, about the journey of life, he sings, 'You think you're happy, think you're free. But maybe we're just comfortably deceived'. It features a keyboard interlude and – oh my God, what's this? – a bass solo. Brown makes his recorded debut with the band, adding some well-placed guitar licks. The track has an urban feel that fits with the sound of most of the rest of the album but still offers every band member a chance to stand out.

'Red Carpet Massacre' (Duran Duran, Hills)
On the title track, the listener gets Duran Duran-turned-punk for a rocking, less than three-and-a-half-minute salvo that also draws inspiration from the Normal's 'Warm Leatherette'. The song focuses on celebrities who seek to take each other down amid a 'battle of the lenses' conducted by a paparazzi death squad. 'Maybe you think you're above this', Le Bon sings. 'But baby we know that you love it'. This Timbaland experiment sounds fairly good after two solid rock-oriented tracks. Maybe the band knew what they were doing?

'Nite-Runner' (Duran Duran, Tim Mosley, Timberlake, Hills)
On the third track, the album briefly goes off the rails, no thanks to Mosley (aka Timbaland) and Timberlake, who make their debut on the album. The song begins with the inane lines, 'You're nocturnal. Only come out at night', and it doesn't get much better from there. When beatbox-style backup vocals kick in and Le Bon starts singing about getting his 'hands on' this nocturnal creature, it's a tad cringeworthy.

Throughout the song, Rhodes' often complex, layered synth work has seemingly been replaced by a couple of notes played on a keyboard. In addition to the beatboxing, Timberlake sings along with Le Bon in the chorus, their vocals melding together to sound more like the r&b singer than the band's own lead vocalist. Timbaland also features on the track, his droning spoken-word vocals dominating the bridge.

The song is an adequate nightclub banger but ultimately doesn't really resemble Duran Duran's classic sound. However, the track features the trademark Timbaland beats that make it sound more like a Timberlake song than 'Falling Down', so perhaps 'Nite-Runner' could have been a hit if it had been released as a single. Fortunately for the band and their legacy, it wasn't.

'Falling Down' (Duran Duran, Timberlake)
Released as a single in November 2007. Chart place: UK: 52
Timberlake produced the album's sole single, a mediocre track inspired by Spears and other female celebrities who had 'fallen down' in full view of the public, including actor Lindsay Lohan and singer Amy Winehouse, who tragically died in 2011.

The song was an attempt to write a ballad in the vein of 'Ordinary World', one of Timberlake's favourite Duran Duran songs. Although Brown's Jimmy Hendrix-style guitar adds some energy to the track, it falls woefully short of their 1990s hit. Le Bon has stated that the song's subject is a motorbike crash he experienced. However, a lyric such as 'And why has my life gone astray? Scarred by disgrace, I know that it's over' seems like a dramatic way to describe a non-fatal accident.

The video, directed by Anthony Mandler, didn't help the song's chart performance, and a clip featuring Timberlake could have given the single the boost it needed. Instead, the band members play doctors in a rehabilitation hospital populated by young models dressed in couture, including one resembling Spears. The muted colour scheme and the focus on the models instead of the band don't make the video any more memorable, though an R-rated version apparently exists in which some of the women appear topless.

'Box Full O' Honey' (Duran Duran, Hills)
This short and sweet ballad is one of the best songs on the album. Acoustic guitar and Le Bon's vocals stand out on the simple track, on which, refreshingly, a single hip-hop beat cannot be heard. Instead, the listener is treated to understated synths and an organic-sounding bassline. Le Bon uses a rather old-fashioned word to describe flirting as he coyly sings about a 'Miss Melancholy': 'Is she dallying with me now?' Although the track couldn't be more different from the one that follows, the transition between the two – the first ending with acoustic guitar and the second beginning with a bass-driven groove – works like a charm.

'Skin Divers' (Duran Duran, Mosley, Hills)
After the album's quietest moment, a Timbaland groove kicks in, joined by Taylor's bass. The track takes off from there as Le Bon opts to sing and wisely leaves the rapping to the actual rapper. The lyrics are dark and quirky, with lines like 'Google dirty fingers' and 'I've misplaced my future can I please borrow yours?', which help to make the track a Duran Duran song featuring Timbaland, rather than the other way around. The song could have easily been taken over by the producer, but aside from the awkward beatbox-style backup vocals during Timbaland's chorus, it's a successful attempt at a Duran Duran song that still retains the album's urban feel.

'Tempted' (Duran Duran, Hills)
This up-tempo track successfully melds Duran Duran's sound with Hills' urban beats and is perfectly suited for the dance floor. Le Bon offers a cool shout-out to his hometown of London and one of his band's biggest hits ('coming undone'). The synth sounds resemble those heard on Timberlake's 'SexyBack', whose creation Hills also had a hand in. But thankfully, Le Bon's vocals aren't distorted as Timberlake's are on that song, making this a fine attempt at modern-day disco-pop.

'Tricked Out' (Duran Duran, Hills)
This instrumental is another decent song on which Rhodes adds layers of synths and Brown shines on guitar. It was one of the only tracks from *Red Carpet Massacre* revived by the band and Mark Ronson during their 2008 live showcase, which proved pivotal for their sound going forward, as it led to future collaborations with the musician and producer. Band members have stated that the song was inspired by punk rock, which Ronson apparently recognised when he used it in a mash-up with Blur's punk-flavoured 'Song 2'.

'Zoom In' (Duran Duran, Mosley, Hills)
This track is about Second Life, a 3D virtual world in which there's a Duran Duran 'Universe'. While the concept hadn't quite caught on in 2007 and their universe wasn't even ready then, the band and Hills still wrote a song about the burgeoning metaverse. Rhodes' spacey synths and Brown's noise guitar add interest to the odd tie-in track, which could have been worse but is merely forgettable. 'Going to make some cash with the avatar', Le Bon sings in a particularly awkward line, and later, he actually refers to 'Second Life' by name.

'She's Too Much' (Duran Duran, Hills)
This tender track about Saffron Le Bon, the singer's then-teenage daughter, is one of the highlights of the album. It begins with Brown's soft guitar riff before Simon Le Bon's vocals kick in. 'She's gentle to the touch', he sings. 'She's everything head first'. Later, he adds sweetly, 'I'll be there when the world is coming down upon her'. The song is an example of the grooves not taking over and allowing the band's playing, including Brown's gentle riffs and Rhodes' understated synths, to come through.

'Dirty Great Monster' (Duran Duran, Hills)
'Dirty Great Monster', which doesn't quite fit the overall sound of the album, is a welcome addition to it, nonetheless. It features electric piano and saxophone, capped by a solo from Simon Willescroft, now a long-time member of Duran Duran's touring band. The track is about an abusive subject, 'the elephant in the living room', Rhodes said in 2007, according to DuranDuran.com. Presumably, the abuser (aka 'the dirty great monster') is the 'daddy' mentioned in the chorus. Le Bon goes on to sing about the 'victims in this show' who 'pretend that it's (the monster's) not there'. The song, which is also notable in that it doesn't have a traditional chorus, stands as a dark and moody artistic statement.

'Last Man Standing' (Duran Duran, Hills)
This plodding closing track is heavy on r&b-style synths and has a repetitive chorus. Although Brown adds an interesting element towards the end of the song with a guitar interlude, it's an unremarkable way to end an album, which, at times, could have been a Simon Le Bon solo album. His vocals certainly stand out here and throughout the LP, but the other band members' playing ultimately becomes lost amid the hip-hop producers' beats.

Extra Tracks

'Cry Baby Cry' (Duran Duran, Hills)
This track, which appears on the Japanese release of *Red Carpet Massacre* (and also features on the current edition of the album), is better than nearly half the songs that made the final tracklist in other countries. It's another

commentary on 'tabloid princesses', but this one seems more like a sincere statement from a band who had faced their own share of cruel barbs in their heyday.

The track features some nice acoustic strumming, an ascending synth line and an infectious melody. 'Afraid of dragons in the smoke', Le Bon sings. 'Wanna go rehab but that's a joke'. Ultimately, he delivers a sage piece of advice: 'But it ain't gonna kill you now. It does make you stronger, yeah'.

Although *Red Carpet Massacre* is a mixed bag of an album, it received generally favourable reviews from critics. However, it sold less than its predecessor, suggesting that fans didn't connect with the album at the same level as with *Astronaut* or any of the band's other more organic-sounding LPs.

All You Need Is Now (2011)

Personnel:
Simon Le Bon: vocals
Nick Rhodes: keyboards
John Taylor: bass
Roger Taylor: drums
Additional musicians:
Dom Brown: guitars
Mark Ronson: guitars
Ana Matronic: vocals
Kelis: vocals
Nina Hossain: vocals
Anna Ross: vocals
Tawiah: vocals
The St. Kitts String Octet: strings
Jamie Walton: cello
Recorded at Sphere Studios from February to August 2010
Produced by Mark Ronson and Duran Duran
Engineer: Josh Blair
Record label: Tape Modern/S-Curve Records
Release date: March 2011
Highest chart places: UK: 11, US: 29
Running time: 56:44
Current edition: 2022 BMG CD/LP

Duran Duran were seemingly down and out following *Red Carpet Massacre*, but an exciting development occurred in 2008 that revitalised the band. In July of that year, they performed at a live showcase, the Smirnoff Experience, with Grammy-winning producer Mark Ronson. The band seamlessly segued from 'Notorious' into 'I Don't Want Your Love' mixed with Prince's 'Sign O' The Times' and played 'A View To A Kill' as part of a Bond medley that brought the house down. The performance was pivotal for both the band and Ronson, a kindred spirit capable of pushing them to new heights.

Ronson, a London-born DJ and musician, had worked with some of the hottest names in music, including Amy Winehouse and Robbie Williams, as well as his stepdad's band, Foreigner. But Duranies were about to learn that the super-producer was one of them, too. Ronson proudly called Duran Duran his 'first favourite band' and John Taylor his style icon, had learned to play guitar from albums like *Notorious* and even performed 'The Wild Boys' at a grade school talent show during his youth. In 2014, he described working with his idols to *Medium*:

> It just started like, 'Well, let's get in and do a couple of songs and see what happens.' I think it was the combination of being a good producer, for the

sake of argument, and being such a super-fan of theirs. It is sort of almost knowing what fans of Duran Duran want to hear.

While working with the band on their new LP, Ronson had learned from Rhodes about analogue synths, which, in turn, inspired his next solo project. Mark Ronson & The Business Intl.'s *Record Collection*, which reached number two on the UK albums chart, featured artwork that referenced the *Rio* cover and guest appearances by Le Bon and Rhodes. Meanwhile, amid the sessions with Ronson, the band recorded a disco-inflected cover of 'Boys Keep Swinging' for the album *We Were So Turned On: A Tribute To David Bowie*.

Duran Duran, a band always so focused on the future, were finally ready to fully embrace their past and had found the producer who told them it was okay to do so. Ronson had a simple but brilliant idea for *All You Need Is Now*: let's make the spiritual follow-up to *Rio*. On the new album, he helped co-write most of the tracks, and Dom Brown was brought into the songwriting fold for the first time.

While the LP clearly harks back to *Rio*, it sounds thoroughly modern all at once. Ronson secured collaborations with several guest artists, including fellow Duranie and Scissor Sisters vocalist Ana Matronic, r&b singer Kelis, Arcade Fire's Owen Pallett and Kaiser Chiefs' Nick Hodgson. He also encouraged the band members to bring instruments they had used in the past into the studio, and when Le Bon ran into writer's block, the producer would walk through an art gallery with him until he found inspiration. The singer told *The Hollywood Reporter* in 2010:

He's the first producer who sat down with us and discussed musical direction before we recorded anything. He put so much time into the album. Sometimes, the lyrics just weren't coming to me, and he'd be asleep on the sofa, but we would go out to get fresh air and some new perspective. Once, we went to an art gallery and there was a Venus de Milo figure with her arms around a big mound of second-hand clothing, and I said, 'Write down 'other people's lives'', and he did, and when we got back to the studio, it became a song. He's a fan of the band, he cares very much about what it sounds like and he has a blueprint to turn those ideas and concepts into actual sounds. Mark fits in with Duran Duran the way we fit in with each other. It's like having another member of the band, really.

The abstract album cover, half hot pink and half grey, features a photo taken by Rhodes and treated by the artist Clunie Reid, the band's new 'D' logo in pink, 'Duran Duran' in white block letters at the top and the album title embossed in black lettering across the photo.

At a time when the music industry was reeling, the band elected to release a nine-track version of the new album for download on iTunes in December 2010. An expanded physical release came out the following March on the independent label S-Curve Records in the US and Tape Modern (which had been created by Rhodes and Stephen Duffy for their side project, The Devils) in the UK. As far as record sales were concerned, not being on a major label at the time had its downsides.

However, *All You Need Is Now* stands as one of Duran Duran's most critically acclaimed albums and was well-received by fans, too. In 2011, the band played big US music festivals like South by Southwest and Coachella, had tastemakers like Ronson and filmmaker David Lynch solidly in their corner and possibly had never been cooler.

Chalk it all up to finding the right producer at the right time.

'All You Need Is Now' (Taylor, Taylor, Rhodes, Le Bon, Ronson, Brown)
Released as a single in December 2010
The lead single features wistful lyrics about the band's fans and an innovative synth hook that almost sounds jarring, announcing that Duran Duran were back – and with a new-old sound. John Taylor was back in a big way, too, delivering classic basslines and not forced to play live bass around a pre-recorded groove, as he had on much of the previous album. Le Bon sounds better than he has in years, harmonising with himself and hitting all the high notes in the uplifting chorus. 'Sway in the moon the way you did when you were younger', he sings to his band – and their fans. 'Stay with the music let it play a little longer'. In the bridge, Rhodes adds a more conventional synth line, and Roger Taylor also gets a chance to shine towards the end of the track.

The video, directed by Nick Egan, was filmed at sites around London, including the Tate Modern. It features black-and-white shots of the band posing and performing in a room walled in foil, Le Bon newly bearded. Outside, young people dressed in New Romantic-style clothing make their way to a nightclub. As the cameras follow the band members around town, a bleach-blonde Ronson makes an appearance, Rhodes walks through a cemetery and Roger Taylor visits a record store before clips from the reunion era play. In this energetic video for an equally vibrant song, the band members appear ready for the future while they fondly embrace their past. The clip isn't groundbreaking – Le Bon described it as a 'new austerity video' in its 'making of' featurette – but captures the band at a pivotal moment.

Duran Duran were on a path towards establishing themselves as the cool elder statesmen of synth pop at a time when the world was looking back with great nostalgia at an era they had helped define.

'Blame The Machines' (Taylor, Taylor, Rhodes, Le Bon, Brown)
This track, about the downsides of GPS technology – 'an interactive nightmare show' – is all shimmering synths and experimental sounds, some sequences of which Rhodes played on his Electronic Dream Plant Wasp. John Taylor locks in with Roger Taylor for a driving rhythm, and ITN newsreader Nina Hossain delivers a spoken-word bridge. Le Bon's vocals are yet another

highlight. 'And now there's no way home this love affair is ended', he sings. 'I should have known when I bought into the dream'. It's among a trio of exhilarating tracks that kick-start the album.

'Being Followed' (Taylor, Taylor, Rhodes, Le Bon, Brown)
Another take on technology examines the UK's surveillance culture to thrilling effect. Buzzy synths from Rhodes' EDP Wasp and a guitar riff by Brown open this track, which features his Andy Taylor-esque guitar stabs during yet another soaring chorus, as well as a signature John Taylor bassline. The song builds into the bridge, in which Le Bon sings dramatically, 'In this chamber lit by scandal. You're the bullet in the barrel ... Still I'm calling out'. Sirens blare in the outro to cap this over-the-top statement that's reminiscent of the band's finest early efforts – a new Duran Duran classic on an album full of them.

'Leave A Light On' (Taylor, Taylor, Rhodes, Le Bon, Brown)
This gentle ballad, which was released as a promotional single, was intended to be a modern-day take on 'Save A Prayer'. While it doesn't quite live up to that timeless single, it's beautiful in its own right. As on 'Save A Prayer', the song features a distinctive synth line – played on a Roland V-Synth GT, one of the few digital sounds on the album – which Rhodes also replicates throughout the track using analogue synths.

The song is a more mature take on a romantic rendezvous. In the verse, Le Bon sings in a lower register, 'In comes the morning. I'm stood in my track. Looking at the reasons for me to head back'. Yet instead of simply calling a one-night stand 'paradise' as on 'Save A Prayer', he promises to return, but only if a light is left on. This sense of maturity is a recurring theme on the album.

'Safe (In The Heat Of The Moment)' (Taylor, Taylor, Rhodes, Le Bon, Ronson, Brown, Matronic)
The funky side of the band is on display in this song, which is highlighted by Matronic's rap. The Scissor Sisters vocalist lends sultriness to the proceedings, while Le Bon plays just 'one more reckless man in the rough'. Rhodes adds vibrant synths – from the Jupiter-8 – while the rhythm section lock in for a danceable groove.

Recording the song was more than a dream come true for Matronic: 'It was one of those moments that I was really nudging the ten-year-old inside me, saying, 'Look at this. I bet you had no clue this was gonna be your life, did you?" she told *NewBeats* in 2015. 'To be able to collaborate with people who have literally shaped your aesthetic – it goes beyond dreams.'

'Girl Panic!' (Taylor, Taylor, Rhodes, Le Bon, Ronson, Brown)
Released as a single in April 2011
Duran Duran make a brilliant exclamation with 'Girl Panic!', which emulates 'Girls On Film'. The song, with its classic synth stabs, disco-style drums and

standout bassline, was released as a 7" single for Record Store Day, which included a remix of the track by Lynch.

Le Bon sings about a night of 'general Chelsea mayhem': 'You beg me to get closer, dress falling off your shoulder', he croons. ''Cause now I sense your mission is my coming demolition. And you just hold me under' – a delightful echo of the line 'as she goes under again' in 'Girls On Film'.

The single was accompanied by a spectacular video by director Jonas Åkerlund, which was filmed at The Savoy Hotel in London and features five supermodels as the band members. Unlike other videos in which the models upstage the band, this is exactly the point here. In fact, throughout the nearly ten-minute video, the music is secondary and heard only at times. Naomi Campbell plays Le Bon, Cindy Crawford is John Taylor, Helena Christensen is Roger Taylor, Eva Herzigová is Rhodes and Yasmin Le Bon cheekily plays 'The Guitarist'. The band members are journalists and hotel employees, and the acting is great. The lavish video shoot was a commercial tie-in with Swarovski and *Harper's Bazaar* magazine, which featured the 'Fab Five' on its cover.

'A Diamond In The Mind' (Taylor, Taylor, Rhodes, Le Bon, Ronson, Brown)
This track serves as a bridge between the up-tempo fabulousness of 'Girl Panic!' and the elegant but no less extraordinary song to follow. Pallett, a violinist, conducted a string octet on this track, 'The Man Who Stole A Leopard' and 'Return To Now', and both this and the latter song are based on the melody of the album's title track. The song is mostly instrumental until the end when Le Bon joins in by singing, 'All you need is now'.

'The Man Who Stole A Leopard' (Taylor, Taylor, Rhodes, Le Bon)
This transcendent song is one of Duran Duran's crowning achievements. Conceived as an attempt to remake 'The Chauffeur', one of Ronson's favourite songs, the track goes beyond that, also taking inspiration from the film *The Collector*, as well as The Velvet Underground song 'The Gift'. While 'The Chauffeur' is just as arty, it's essentially a Le Bon/Rhodes production. On the newer track, all hands are on deck. Synths, strings and bass propel the song, which is capped by a synth guitar solo. In call-and-response vocals, Le Bon sings, 'I watch her while she sleeps', as Kelis adds, 'Be sure she dreams of you'. Throughout the track, he repeats the line, 'Don't spill my secret'.

The tale of a man and his beloved wild-animal companion was inspired by a news article, a version of which Hossein reads toward the end of the track in an echo of the nature record sampled on 'The Chauffeur'. As the song fades out, a musical sample from the Nino Rota soundtrack to the Luchino Visconti film *Rocco And His Brothers* plays. The song borders on being pretentious, but – as with much of the band's best music – merely stands out as a stunning artistic statement.

'Other People's Lives' (Taylor, Taylor, Rhodes, Le Bon, Ronson, Brown)
Duran Duran revisit celebrity culture on this track, which was inspired by the Venus de Milo figure viewed by Le Bon and Ronson at an art gallery during the album's recording. The singer thought up the song's title when he saw the sculpture holding second-hand clothing, which could be interpreted as the 'dirty laundry' that's 'everywhere in shocking colour on the page'.

The synth-heavy track's cheeky lyrics also reference media personality Katie Price ('Every Katie's got her price'). 'Read the headlines. Hear the sirens', Le Bon sings about the plight of some 'tabloid princesses', a topic the band also explored on their previous LP. 'Out of rehab again'. John Taylor sings backup in the call-and-response chorus.

'Mediterranea' (Taylor, Taylor, Rhodes, Le Bon, Ronson, Brown)
The sound of waves and music that almost evokes The Beach Boys' 'Kokomo' serves as the introduction to this track. As on much of the album, it showcases a band not taking themselves entirely seriously but still being sincere.

On 'Mediterranea', Duran Duran go on a holiday in the sun – possibly involving a yacht excursion, of course – and this time around, they aren't apologising for their glamorous lifestyle. 'Arriving there in a wave of heat. Lying on the beach tequila mayhem', Le Bon sings. 'Let the sun shine out of your mind'. Brown plays some standout guitar, and Rhodes adds understated synths to complete the laid-back atmosphere. The keyboardist used an analogue synth, the Elka Synthex, to create layers of lovely bell tones throughout the track.

'Too Bad You're So Beautiful' (Taylor, Taylor, Rhodes, Le Bon, Brown, Hodgson)
Hodgson, the drummer for Kaiser Chiefs, helped write this bass-driven song about a 'king of nothing' and 'an ice queen up on the mountain'. In the bridge, Rhodes layers shimmering synths, and Taylor adds a catchy bassline with a flourish towards the end. The track keeps building and doesn't lose steam, fading out as Le Bon repeatedly sings, 'Too bad, just too bad'. This song reminds the listener of one of the band's best early tracks, 'Last Chance On The Stairway', another tale of hopeless romanticism, this time in which Le Bon plays the part of 'a deluded fool' who can't help but be fascinated with his beautiful and complicated love interest.

'Runway Runaway' (Taylor, Taylor, Rhodes, Le Bon, Brown)
An album of standout material perhaps hits its peak with this short and sweet song about a model leaving home to pursue her dream. It's unapologetically Duran Duran and shows that they're not afraid to wear their hearts on their sleeves – or to mine their past. Over the course of three exhilarating minutes, every player has his chance to stand out: John Taylor

delivers a driving bassline, Roger Taylor adds thrilling drum fills, Brown plays some stellar new wave-style guitar, channelling Andy Taylor at times, and Rhodes' synths wash over the track. As on the rest of the album, Le Bon sounds great, especially in the soaring chorus ('Say goodbye, she's not afraid of leaving'). It's a synth pop classic that rivals anything from the slew of younger bands of the era who had sought to emulate Duran Duran's signature sound.

'Return To Now' (Taylor, Taylor, Rhodes, Le Bon, Ronson, Brown)
The LP's second instrumental is a brief but beautiful lead-in to the album's closing track. Both songs feature cellist Jamie Walton.

'Before The Rain' (Taylor, Taylor, Rhodes, Le Bon)
Le Bon tried to rewrite Wolfgang Amadeus Mozart's 'Requiem' but ended up with a stately song about a man's 'ghosts of guilt'. The track, which also brings to mind 'The Chauffeur', begins with Le Bon's poetic lyrics set to Walton's live cello and Rhodes' Fairlight synth until the rest of the band members join in around the two-minute mark. 'And so we travel and we unravel', Le Bon sings, each line marked by a militaristic snare drum. 'Towards the place where all loose ends go'. It's a brilliant artistic statement to close one of the band's best albums in elegant fashion.

Extra Tracks

'Too Close To The Sun' (Taylor, Taylor, Rhodes, Le Bon, Brown)
This song, a bonus track on an edition of the album sold by the US retailer Best Buy, is different from the rest of the material from the *All You Need Is Now* sessions. The track flirts with electronica and features Le Bon's falsetto. Yet, despite its great chorus and some nice guitar riffs, it doesn't quite rise to the level of the 14 tracks that made the album.

'Early Summer Nerves' (Taylor, Taylor, Rhodes, Le Bon, Brown)
The second bonus track on the Best Buy edition is more experimental than the first. The song has a Grace Jones vibe, dominated by synths and throbbing bass. 'Welcome to Miss Adventure. Oh, she is a slippery slope', Le Bon sings, reaching into a higher register throughout the song and even whistling in the outro.

'Networker Nation' (Taylor, Taylor, Rhodes, Le Bon, Brown)
This song, a bonus track on the album, explores technology. It opens with a computerised voice spelling out 'Duran Duran' and includes references to Facebook and YouTube, which could have dated the song, but the platforms are still as prescient as ever. 'Elegant times for no conversation', Le Bon sings. ''Cause now we're online. A networker nation'. The high-energy track features layers of synths and some great guitar work by Brown.

'This Lost Weekend' (Taylor, Taylor, Rhodes, Le Bon, Brown)
Rhodes likens the sound of this song, which appears on the deluxe edition of the vinyl LP, to Motown. As with the other bonus tracks, this one is quite different from the songs on the 14-track album. It consists mostly of Le Bon's vocals and Brown's guitar.

Wisely, the band saved their experimentation for the extra tracks, which are still good songs but don't live up to the quality of those that made the album. With *All You Need Is Now*, Duran Duran triumphantly reclaimed their past – and haven't let go.

Paper Gods (2015)

Personnel:
Simon Le Bon: vocals
Nick Rhodes: keyboards
John Taylor: bass
Roger Taylor: drums
Additional musicians:
Nile Rodgers: guitars
John Frusciante: guitars
Dom Brown: guitars
Mr Hudson: vocals
Kiesza: vocals
Janelle Monáe: vocals
Lindsay Lohan: vocals
Jonas Bjerre: vocals
Hollie Cook: vocals
Anna Ross: vocals
Voce Chamber Choir: vocals
London Youth Chamber Choir: vocals
Davide Rossi: strings
Recorded at Battersea Park Studios from 2013 to 2015
Produced by Duran Duran, Mr Hudson, Mark Ronson, Nile Rodgers and Josh Blair
Engineer: Josh Blair
Record label: Warner Bros. Records
Release date: September 2015
Highest chart places: UK: 5, US: 10
Running time: 57:21
Current edition: 2015 Warner Bros. CD/LP

Duran Duran had re-established and reinvigorated themselves with *All You Need Is Now*, an album of thrilling tracks with nary a piece of filler. They followed that success with an extensive run of live shows, two of which were filmed professionally.

The first was *Duran Duran: Unstaged*, a live online performance that was later released in movie theatres in North America and on DVD. The band landed a dream gig when they teamed up with groundbreaking filmmaker David Lynch and American Express for the show just days after the physical release of *All You Need Is Now*. The concert was chock-full of unique visuals and musical guests. In addition to familiar collaborators Mark Ronson and Kelis, they were also joined by My Chemical Romance's Gerard Way on 'Planet Earth' and Gossip's Beth Ditto on 'Notorious'.

However, the *All You Need Is Now* tour was not without its scary moments. Duran Duran were forced to cancel a string of shows in Europe when Le Bon suffered a haemorrhage on his vocal cords. Unlike his vocal scare in the early 1990s, this time, fans witnessed, via the internet, the unravelling of a tour date by date. There was uncertainty over whether this meant the end of the band, but slowly, he regained his voice. The band opened up their UK rehearsal shows for the next batch of live dates to fans and released a film and an album of their concert in Manchester from the tour that followed. *A Diamond In The Mind: Live 2011* captured the band back in top form, playing a tight and blistering set.

In 2012, they delivered a triumphant performance at Hyde Park to celebrate the opening of the London Summer Olympic Games, Le Bon proudly donning a Union Jack blazer designed by Antony Price. Later in the year, John Taylor looked back on his past with the release of his autobiography, *In The Pleasure Groove: Love, Death & Duran Duran*, which became an international best-seller.

As buzz began to swirl about a new Duran Duran album, Rhodes finally released material from TV Mania, his avant-garde project with Warren Cuccurullo, titled *Bored With Prozac And The Internet?*

Meanwhile, the band announced that their next project would move them 'closer to the dance floor' and that Ronson would co-produce the new material. At Ronson's suggestion, Nile Rodgers was brought into the fold as well. The super-producers had admired one another's music but had never worked together before. Rodgers felt like he had come home: 'It makes it feel to me like I'm back with my band in a way', he said on the *Paper Gods* electronic press kit. 'All the guys in my original band, Chic, have all passed away. So, I feel like Duran Duran are my second band.'

The Duranie duo ended up being credited as producers on only two of the album's tracks, as the band also hooked up with yet another collaborator. Benjamin Hudson McIldowie (aka 'Mr Hudson') – a pop and hip-hop producer, musician and songwriter – also hailed from Birmingham and had big love for his fellow Brummies. He went on to play a key role in the band's musical direction in the years to come. As Rhodes told *Time* magazine in 2015, 'We're a tough room – we've known each other for over three and a half decades. You [Hudson] walk in and we think, 'Alright, what are you going to do? Impress us!' And he actually did!'

Paper Gods marked a move towards modern, dance-oriented sounds after the new wave authenticity of *All You Need Is Now*. In addition to working with the trio of hot producers, the band brought in several guest artists, including Canadian singer Kiesza, Red Hot Chili Peppers guitarist John Frusciante, Mew vocalist Jonas Bjerre and actor Lindsay Lohan. On the first single, 'Pressure Off', Le Bon was joined on vocals by the biggest name of them all, r&b singer and actor Janelle Monáe, along with Rodgers on guitar.

'Pressure Off' mirrored a shift in the music industry towards collaborations. Since last working with Duran Duran, Rodgers and Ronson had teamed up with hip acts to huge success. Rodgers helped lead a funk revival with French electronic duo Daft Punk on their Grammy-winning album *Random Access Memories* and its smash single 'Get Lucky' featuring Pharrell Williams. Ronson went on to collect Grammys for the song 'Uptown Funk', featuring Bruno Mars, from the producer's solo album *Uptown Special*. The engineer of the latter track, Josh Blair, who had served as the engineer on *All You Need Is Now*, was back on board with Duran Duran as engineer. And despite all the big-name collaborators, Blair is credited as the sole co-producer of the majority of the songs on *Paper Gods* and all its bonus tracks. Still, the excitement surrounding the high-profile collaborations was no doubt a factor when the band signed a global recording contract with major label Warner Bros. Records after the album's completion.

The *Paper Gods* cover, by artist Alex Israel, references images from the band's past, including 'stickers' depicting a 'cherry ice cream smile', a sumo wrestler and a tiger. Even though the LP lacked the cohesiveness of its predecessor, it highlighted the eclectic energy that's present in much of the band's work. The album's cover and its better tracks showed that Duran Duran were capable of making a classic with a modern spin. As Ronson told *Grantland* in 2015:

> They're four guys that, as you can imagine, have four different tastes in music, but where they meet in the middle just happens to be a place of impeccably good taste. There's no desperate sense of cool-hunting or trying to stay relevant.

The album was released to general critical and commercial acclaim, becoming the band's first LP to crack the *Billboard* top ten since *The Wedding Album*, as well as being a top-five hit in the UK. With its success in the US came the opportunity to play bigger venues in the country, even outside larger markets, often with Nile Rodgers & Chic in tow.

Paper Gods, with its solid chart performance, stands as an important album, as it helped bring the band back into the public consciousness, paving the way to further honours in the years to come.

'Paper Gods' (Taylor, Taylor, Rhodes, Le Bon, Hudson)
The lead-off track has been described by John Taylor as a 'journey song' in the vein of 'The Valley'. It starts quietly with Hudson's a cappella vocals before a dance floor beat kicks in. Le Bon, in rapid-fire succession, then delivers lyrics that take on the 'paper gods' and the exploitation of people like 'the slaver in a sweatshop putting trainers on your feet'. While he determines that the 'fools in town are ruling now' and even that 'the total human race became a basket case', he cheekily adds, 'It's nothing to lose face about, it's really not our place to doubt it'. Despite the serious topic, the song features a soaring chorus and sparkling synths – Rhodes used an Alesis Andromeda on this song and elsewhere on the album – combining darkness and light in

Duran Duran's trademark fashion. It's a solid musical statement to open an ambitious album.

'Last Night In The City' (Taylor, Taylor, Rhodes, Le Bon, Kiesza, Mr Hudson)
Released as a single in March 2017
After starting the album respectably with its title track, Duran Duran launch into 'Last Night In The City', an EDM-influenced song that begins with the vocals of Canadian songstress Kiesza before Le Bon joins in. He pushes his voice to the limit on the track, which was co-produced by Hudson and Blair. Though Taylor often blends synth and live bass, he played only synth bass on this song. So, the track, being devoid of a traditional bassline and standout synth work, ultimately doesn't sound much like Duran Duran, save for Le Bon's vocals. Oddly, the band chose to release a video for the song a year after the album came out and the single over a year later, perhaps aiming for a late-breaking hit on the dance charts.

The video, directed by Nick Egan and Snorri Brothers, features the band performing live with Kiesza. Stylistically, it resembles videos of its time that appeared on shows like *MTV Clubland*, the channel's dance music hour. It also includes shots of the band's travels during the *Paper Gods* tour – after all, Le Bon and Kiesza sing, 'I've been travelling around now, big world with my brothers' in one of the song's better lines. However, ultimately, the video and the single in general just aren't very impressive coming from a band of Duran Duran's calibre.

'You Kill Me With Silence' (Taylor, Taylor, Rhodes, Le Bon, Mr Hudson)
This song, the band's first recorded with Hudson, is lyrically interesting and musically experimental. It opens with synths and a trap beat before Le Bon launches into the clever lyrics about a woman who is killing him with silence. He references Bowie ('To drive another lad insane') and delivers stinging lines such as, 'I like this bed of nails ... Couldn't be much worse in hell'. The song builds in intensity and is capped by what sounds like incendiary guitar, but which is actually a synth solo by Rhodes, played on the Elka Synthex. 'It's sort of all my guitar envy coming out in a solo!' he told *Keyboard* magazine in 2015.

'Pressure Off' (Taylor, Taylor, Rhodes, Le Bon, Rodgers, Ronson, Mr Hudson, Monáe)
Released as a single in June 2015
The album's first single – co-produced by Rodgers, Ronson and Hudson – features Rodgers' funk guitar, Rhodes' synth riffs, an infectious beat and Monáe's standout vocals. The singer dominates the chorus and the final verse, her voice fitting surprisingly well within the band's sound. The simple yet effective lyrics are a call for fans to 'step out into the future' with Duran Duran – or just an invitation to take the pressure off and dance along to a

band 'designed to make you party', as Le Bon has proclaimed. The track ends with roaring applause, just as during their live shows.

The video, a fine directing effort from Egan, features both Rodgers and Monáe. Due to the logistics of getting all the players on board for the clip, its release was delayed, and it arrived four months after the single dropped. The band members, Rodgers and Monáe, who were filmed separately but appear to be performing together, leap into the air against a stark white background – visuals inspired by the work of photographer Philippe Halsman. They're all smiles, shining brightly, even in black and white. Egan has called 'Pressure Off' his favourite video. It's certainly a crisp, modern and effective clip for a joyful song.

'Face For Today' (Taylor, Taylor, Rhodes, Le Bon, Brown)
The album keeps building in momentum with the first of several songs co-produced by Blair. 'Face For Today' is as electronic as any song on the album, yet it manages to sound like vintage Duran Duran. Instead of chasing the EDM trend, they add a modern electronic sheen to their new wave sound on the track, which features loads of shimmering synths (including from the Jupiter-8), live strings and a driving bassline – a combination of synth bass and live bass, which was processed and reversed.

The song was accompanied by a video, which was directed by Rhodes' daughter, Tatjana, and released as a thank-you to the band's fans. It's essentially a compilation of photos of Duranies submitted by the fans themselves, to which the band added a tagline with lyrics from the song: 'You've got that thing which makes us smile.'

'Danceophobia' (Taylor, Taylor, Rhodes, Le Bon, Brown, Mr Hudson)
As on several latter-day Duran Duran albums, *Paper Gods* contains a dud, this one featuring Lohan's spoken-word vocal. She unconvincingly plays a doctor who diagnoses someone – perhaps a listener resistant to the song itself – with 'Danceophobia'. While the track is intended to be cheeky and fun, it's musically flimsy with its EDM-style synths and lyrical repetitiveness. As for Lohan, the actor doesn't add much to the project other than the recognition associated with her name. The band worked on at least 60 different versions of the song, indicating that they had overthought a piece of music that should have just been simple and fun.

'What Are The Chances?' (Taylor, Taylor, Rhodes, Le Bon, Brown, Mr Hudson)
The album gets back on track in a big way with this lovely ballad, which features live strings by Davide Rossi, as well as standout guitar from John Frusciante, who channels Warren Cuccurullo at times. The collaboration came about after the Red Hot Chili Peppers guitarist reached out to the band, saying he was a long-time fan and wanted to play on their new album. 'You

can't say no to John Frusciante', Roger Taylor told *Yellow Scene Magazine* in 2015. 'He's probably one of the greatest living guitar players, in our eyes anyway.'

Le Bon harmonises with himself beautifully and raises questions about fate in the tender lyrics. 'Playing with your life, or is it destiny which sets you on a path?' he asks. 'Is it out of choice that you're here next to me, or just the aftermath of moments as they pass?' His soaring vocals, Frusciante's guitar and the lush strings bring to mind 'Ordinary World' – and both ballads are among the band's best.

'Sunset Garage' (Taylor, Taylor, Rhodes, Le Bon, Mr Hudson)
This uplifting song, co-produced by Hudson and Blair, is driven by the rhythm section, with drums inspired by Electric Light Orchestra. 'The chorus on this song is just JT and me doing our thing', Roger Taylor told *Modern Drummer* in 2015. The highlight is the instrumental break, in which the bass takes centre stage before Le Bon adds a wistful line to the otherwise cheery track: 'Yesterday looks so tame, so far away from this point of disarray'. Overall, it's a bubbly burst of nostalgia that leaves EDM behind for a moment.

'Change The Skyline' (Taylor, Taylor, Rhodes, Le Bon, Mr Hudson)
This song was originally intended to feature Brandon Flowers of The Killers, but when that collaboration didn't come to fruition, Jonas Bjerre of Mew stepped in to add his distinctive falsetto to the track. The up-tempo song features Daft Punk-esque synths and an anthemic chorus. While the track is a pleasant enough listen, it doesn't seem as fully formed as most of the album's songs and peters out towards the end.

'Butterfly Girl' (Taylor, Taylor, Rhodes, Le Bon, Brown)
One of the album's deep tracks features funky guitar from Frusciante, along with Brown, who is also credited as a co-writer of this song and several others on the LP. Le Bon steps aside at times to let London-born backup singer Anna Ross take a star turn with her Chic-esque vocals, and the two singers' voices also work well together. The song, about a woman 'adrift in [her] own sympathy' who finds 'only one kind of happy in that glass of wine', is a funky, rocking track that kicks off a solid trio to close the album.

'Only In Dreams' (Taylor, Taylor, Rhodes, Le Bon, Rodgers, Ronson, Mr Hudson)
The album's other track co-produced by Rodgers, Ronson and Hudson is a hypnotic foray into 1980s funk, featuring poetic lyrics by Le Bon and guitar from Rodgers. As the music – boosted by bass, octaver and synth bass – takes the listener on a trippy, thrilling ride, Le Bon paints a dreamlike picture. 'There's a vampire in the limousine', he sings. 'Sun's going down like a symphony', to which he adds the quirky line: 'She keeps her guard up

while her nails are wet'. The song is one of the album's best and fits well with the band's classic sound.

'The Universe Alone' (Taylor, Taylor, Rhodes, Le Bon)
The closing track, perhaps the album's finest, is a ballad fit for the apocalypse. Frusciante's funky guitar, Taylor's solid bassline, Rhodes' soaring synths and Roger Taylor's syncopated drumming are the perfect accompaniment for Le Bon's beautiful vocals and lyrics. Rossi's strings and the sound of two choirs add classical elements to the song, which ends with a modern twist as the drumming becomes distorted before a cappella voices draw the LP to an epic close, similar to how it began.

The song has been described as a take on Frank Sinatra's 'My Way'. While the crooner sang that 'the end is near', he stayed within his own orbit. However, Le Bon goes further into the universe to tell a tale of 'the end of everything and everyone'. The first line of the song alone – 'It's beautiful the dying sun' – is a striking way to open the darkly gorgeous track, which stands out as one of the band's best latter-day album closers.

Extra Tracks

'Planet Roaring' (Taylor, Taylor, Rhodes, Le Bon, Brown)
This intense song, a bonus track on the deluxe edition of the album, features Sex Pistol and John Taylor's Notorious Outsiders bandmate Steve Jones on guitar and standout backup vocals by Ross. In the anthemic lyrics, Le Bon sings, perhaps of the band, 'We carry on. We are the song' before he concludes with an apt description for the track itself: 'It's the sound of celebration'.

'Valentine Stones' (Taylor, Taylor, Rhodes, Le Bon)
This synth-heavy song, another bonus track on the deluxe version of the LP, is better than some that made the 12-track album – notably 'Last Night In The City' and 'Danceophobia' – and it turns out that it almost did make the cut. Accompanied by thumping bass and a danceable beat, Le Bon sings, 'I don't want to be like the boys that you keep in tow. Like your valentine stones'. It's a sultry, funky track that's reminiscent of some from *The Wedding Album* era.

'Northern Lights' (Taylor, Taylor, Rhodes, Le Bon, Brown)
The sounds of footsteps on snowy ground start this experimental song, a bonus track that appears on the deluxe edition of the album and features Frusciante and Brown on guitar, as well as live strings. Le Bon tells the subject, who's 'got a thing that I care about', that 'If you want to stay tonight. Write your name across the sky', perhaps evoking a love interest as awe-inspiring as the Northern Lights themselves. He sings in a higher register throughout the song, which is yet another solid bonus track.

'On Evil Beach' (Taylor, Taylor, Rhodes, Le Bon)
This bonus track on the version of the album sold by the US retailer Target is a short, synth-heavy song with cryptic lyrics that reference sharks that 'swim to the pool' and a preacher who 'sighs in four dimensions'. It's one of the more experimental tracks to come out of the *Paper Gods* sessions but also one of the least impressive.

'Cinderella Ride' (Taylor, Taylor, Rhodes, Le Bon, Brown)
This track, which also appeared on the deluxe edition of the LP sold by Target, features Rhodes' synthesiser flourishes, Brown's understated guitar and a chorus befitting a classic new wave song. Le Bon implores the subject, perhaps the folk tale character Cinderella, who ascended to royalty herself, to become a 'queen of helpless things' by riding with him 'out into a smoke-filled night across The Bridge of Tears, where children with their eyes sewn shut lay begging on the stones'. 'We will lead them home', he sings, suggesting that she can provide aid to the helpless. This interpretation also evokes the late Princess Diana, who was known for her philanthropy. Taylor and Rhodes shine on the track, especially during its instrumental outro. With its mix of serious lyrics and uplifting music, this song fits well alongside several others in Duran Duran's catalogue.

'As Seen From A Distance' (Taylor, Taylor, Rhodes, Le Bon)
This bonus track on the limited-edition vinyl box set of the album is mainly an instrumental, which features Le Bon only as he sings the title, followed by the line 'the death of a killer'. The song has some nice synth work and a driving drum beat, but with its spare lyrics, it just seems like an unfinished jam.

Overall, with *Paper Gods*, Duran Duran managed to deliver a solid batch of bonus tracks, in addition to an album that made many critics take notice.

Future Past (2021)

Personnel:
Simon Le Bon: vocals
Nick Rhodes: keyboards
John Taylor: bass
Roger Taylor: drums
Additional musicians:
Graham Coxon: guitars
Mark Ronson: guitars
Georgio Moroder: keyboards
Mike Garson: piano
Erol Alkan: programming
Josh Blair: string arrangements, piano, guitar
Tove Lo: vocals
Ivorian Doll: vocals
Chai: vocals
Barli: vocals
Saffron Le Bon: vocals
Recorded at Assault & Battery Studios and Tape Modern Studios from 2018 to 2021
Produced by Erol Alkan, Duran Duran, Giorgio Moroder and Josh Blair
Engineer: Josh Blair
Record label: BMG/Tape Modern
Release date: October 2021
Highest chart places: UK: 3, US: 28
Running time: 60:47 (deluxe edition)
Current edition: 2021 BMG CD/2022 BMG LP

Duran Duran had moderate success with *Paper Gods*, scoring solidly on the charts in the UK and the US; Le Bon proudly announced the top-ten *Billboard* placement onstage at Red Rocks Amphitheatre outside Denver, Colorado, during a promotional tour for the album's release. The band toured extensively in support of the LP, especially in the US. Notably, in 2016, Rhodes left the tour due to a family emergency and was replaced by electronic artist and Mark Ronson collaborator MNDR, resulting in a rare stint of live performances without the keyboardist.

In 2017, they recorded a show in Japan, which was released on vinyl as *Duran Duran Budokan* for Record Store Day the following year. Also in 2018, they 'took over' BBC Four for an evening of programming, including episodes of *Top Of The Pops* featuring the band, the *Unstaged* concert film, the special *A Night In* and a new documentary, *There's Something You Should Know* – all to mark the band's 40th anniversary.

As they continued to tour into 2019, they played a concert at NASA's Kennedy Space Center in Florida to mark the anniversary of the Apollo 11 mission, performing a space-themed setlist that began with 'The Universe Alone', which was accompanied by a spine-tingling drone show. Earlier that year, Le Bon and John Taylor had the immense honour of inducting their heroes, Roxy Music, into the Rock & Roll Hall of Fame. During their speech, Le Bon described Roxy as 'pulp science fiction' and Taylor recounted seeing them live for the first time in Birmingham when he was 14, a performance he recorded on a portable cassette player:

> The next night, in my darkened suburban bedroom, I listened back and realised what I wanted to be. I knew my destiny ... [Brian] Eno once said of The Velvet Underground, 'They didn't sell many records, but everyone who bought one formed a band.' Roxy sold many more records than The Velvet Underground, and they influenced the life choices of everyone who came into contact with them ... I am always proud to say that without Roxy Music, there really would be no Duran Duran.

Le Bon and Taylor looked every bit the handsome elder statesmen of new wave and elicited many cheers themselves during the speech, which was a key moment that set them on their own path to recognition. Since *Paper Gods*, the band had amassed several other honours, including a Q Icon Award, an MTV Europe Music Awards Visionary Award and an ASCAP Golden Note Award.

Meanwhile, they returned to the studio, joined by collaborators including Ronson, producer Erol Alkan, guitarist Graham Coxon and Swedish singer Lykke Li. Ronson, his own star rising ever higher, ended up being credited as a co-writer and guitarist on only one song on the album, and the Li collaboration remains unreleased.

Alkan – a Londoner best known as a DJ and a producer for acts including The Killers and Ride – had suggested bringing in his neighbour, Coxon, who became like a fifth member of the band during the recording and initial promotion of the album. Alkan proclaimed himself a long-time fan of Duran Duran, and their influence also could be heard in the music of Coxon's band Blur, especially on songs like 'Girls & Boys'. As Roger Taylor told *Classic Pop* in 2021:

> Graham has been a pop star himself for 30 years, so we didn't know how much ego he'd bring with him. But he was humble and funny, a lovely guy. He's the perfect Duran Duran guitarist because, as well as his own talent, he can morph into playing like all of David Bowie's different guitarists. Graham can give up a bit of Robert Fripp, Mick Ronson, Nile Rodgers.

The band initially began working on *Future Past* well before the COVID-19 pandemic struck in 2020 but held off on releasing the album until they could support it with live shows. Most of the songs' lyrics were written prior to the pandemic but ended up being prescient in its aftermath, notably on the first single, 'Invisible'. (Both Le Bon and Taylor had fallen ill with the virus early on.) As social distancing became the new normal, the band began taking part in performances remotely, including *A Bowie Celebration*, a live-streamed tribute concert to mark the fifth anniversary of the singer's death, in early 2021. They performed 'Five Years' with the event's organiser, Bowie pianist Mike Garson, who was also a guest artist on *Future Past*.

The album featured additional collaborations. For the first time, they worked with disco innovator Giorgio Moroder, who co-produced and played keyboards on two tracks. Josh Blair was also back as a co-producer and engineer. Other guest stars were more unexpected: Swedish singer-songwriter Tove Lo, London rapper Ivorian Doll and Japanese pop-punk band Chai. Most of the recording sessions took place at Assault & Battery Studios, a small outfit in London owned by two other big-name producers: Alan Moulder and Flood.

In the fall of 2021, six years after their last album, Duran Duran finally released *Future Past* via Tape Modern/BMG. A changed world resulted in a changed album; Rhodes said the band members revisited the material they had recorded before the pandemic, listening to it with fresh ears after time away from the studio. The album's cover features images by Japanese photographer Daisuke Yokoto; artist Rory McCartney combined two of Yokoto's black-and-white photos and colourised them in red and green.

Future Past was successful both critically and commercially, especially in the UK, where the album became the band's second straight LP to crack the top five. It briefly battled for the top spot with a new release from Elton John and landed at number three, behind John and singer Lana Del Ray.

The album dropped at a time when success on the pop charts meant much less than it once did. *Future Past* boasted several singles, all of them released digitally. 'Invisible' became the biggest hit of the lot due to its unexpected popularity with young gamers, who have made it one of the band's most-streamed songs of all time.

However, the biggest impact of *Future Past*, like the two albums before it, was on the band's enduring legacy. Duran Duran had lasted 40 years and counting and were still putting out relevant music. That's no small feat, and critics – as well as rock's most hallowed institution – were certainly taking notice.

'Invisible' (Taylor, Taylor, Rhodes, Le Bon, Alkan)
Released as a single in May 2021
The album begins on a high note with the first single, a strong pop funk jam. The track opens with a Prince-esque guitar riff and a whispered backup vocal, which may be the only quiet thing about the song. The band members produce a wall of sound with Taylor's funky bass, Rhodes' equally funky keyboards, Roger Taylor's powerful electronic drums and Coxon's slicing guitar riffs. Le Bon's vocals are strong as he delivers lyrics that focus on a shy,

'quiet one' who is 'silently ignored'. But in the final chorus, he proclaims that 'a voiceless crowd isn't backing down'. 'Have we all become invisible?' he asks at the end. The song is among several on the album whose lyrics address emotions and intimacy on a personal scale while also being open to a more universal interpretation – music for the masses.

The eerie video, by AI 'director' Huxley, was touted by the band as the 'first collaboration of its kind between artists in different planes of existence'. It features close-up shots of the band members' faces as they mouth the song's lyrics, merging into other haunting, dreamlike, blurred images.

The song became a streaming smash when it gained popularity in the *Metal Gear* and *Fortnite* gaming communities on TikTok after being used for 'edits' featuring a character called Solid Snake.

'All Of You' (Taylor, Taylor, Rhodes, Le Bon, Coxon)
The album really takes off with this track, a lyrical love letter set to a dance floor beat. Rhodes' synths bubble over the track as Coxon channels Fripp with his guitar riff following the chorus and John Taylor adds a killer bassline, locking in with Roger Taylor, whose drumming on the album is among his strongest in years. Le Bon again delivers vocally, with heartfelt lyrics about his own relationship with his wife of more than 35 years, Yasmin. 'We are music lovers. This much we've learnt', he sings. 'Two souls among many others. Like the sun we burn'. The tender, effervescent track is an instant Duran Duran classic.

The song, which could have been another strong single, was released on vinyl in the form of an extended 'rework' by Alkan. The nod to the band's beloved 'Night Versions' highlighted the vocals of backup singer Barli.

'Give It All Up' (Taylor, Taylor, Rhodes, Le Bon, Alkan, Coxon, Lo)
Swirling synths wash over this track as Lo's vocals meld seamlessly with those of Le Bon. The vocalists trade verses and join together in the chorus, backed by a throbbing dance beat. The bittersweet lyrics address two lovers who try to remain dedicated to one another despite having grown apart. 'The moon looks down on broken vows, fills the space between us with cold blue shine', Lo sings. 'And I can't remember how our love felt at the start'.

An extended rework of the song by Alkan was also released on vinyl.

'Anniversary' (Taylor, Taylor, Rhodes, Le Bon, Alkan, Coxon)
Released as a single in August 2021
The party really gets started with this infectious piece of nostalgia about the band's big anniversary. It opens with a bassline reminiscent of 'The Wild Boys' and Le Bon's invitation to 'come celebrate this union' and features female backup vocals that bring to mind 'The Reflex' – 'Easter eggs, for the fans to find', John Taylor said in a statement in 2021. Le Bon strains a bit to reach the high notes in the chorus, which he has admitted is out of his range. But the

song is lyrically strong, especially in its synth-soaked bridge. 'It may not seem like much at all', Le Bon sings. 'But it's everything to us'. The outro is another highlight, on which he seemingly ad-libs his vocals, which are capped by a shout-out to INXS' 'Need You Tonight' with 'All we have is this moment, yeah'.

While the song is a look back, it's also a statement about the band's enduring relevancy, with lines like 'Across the world on radio for anyone to hear. We are the song, so bring it on'. Indeed, three of the album's first four tracks were added to BBC Radio 2's A-List.

The video for the song, directed by Alison Jackson, features Duran Duran as guests at a wild, lavish party at Belvoir Castle in Leicestershire, also attended by various 'celebrities' as well as actors playing the band members in their younger days. The over-the-top production includes cheeky scenes featuring a poker game between a Queen Elizabeth impersonator, Le Bon and Rhodes and several appearances by 'Daniel Craig' and, disturbingly, 'Vladimir Putin'. Other famous people depicted in the clip include Madonna, Elton John, Lady Gaga and Kim Kardashian.

'Future Past' (Taylor, Taylor, Rhodes, Le Bon, Alkan, Coxon)
The title track is a soaring ballad that features what sounds like sleigh bells, which evoke the festive season for some listeners. But rather than coming off as a Christmas tune, the song just warms like a fireplace on a cold winter day. Again, Le Bon's lyrics and vocals are highlights, especially as he reaches into the lower end of his register in the verse. 'This life is not to our design. Could not have known it then, but now I see it plain', he sings. On the track, a reflection on life and mistakes of the past, Coxon even channels Andy Taylor circa *Seven And The Ragged Tiger* with his guitar solo.

'Velvet Newton' (Taylor, Taylor, Rhodes, Le Bon, Coxon)
This mostly instrumental track is one of the band's best of its kind. It begins with the apt line 'This is how it starts' before spacey synths and booming bass kick in. Le Bon is nearly unintelligible as he repeatedly sings, 'It can feel normal. Feel all around', and Coxon adds buzzy guitar. It ends with what sounds like a spaceship blasting off. The song opened the *Future Past* tour, accompanied by a video in which avatars of the band members are seen landing on Earth, fittingly, via a spaceship.

'Beautiful Lies' (Taylor, Taylor, Rhodes, Le Bon, Moroder)
Although the pairing of the band and Moroder should have been a match made in heaven, the two tracks they produced together come up short. 'Beautiful Lies', the better effort of the two, features a funky combo of synth and live bass and backup vocals by Le Bon's daughter Saffron. The vocalist, once the subject of the song 'She's Too Much', takes a star turn with her performance on this track and several others. The vocals of father and daughter meld beautifully, similar to how Le Bon harmonises so wonderfully with himself. Blair adds

understated guitar to the song, which is danceable and fun, especially with Duran Duran-esque lyrics such as 'You taste like cherry ice'.

'Tonight United' (Taylor, Taylor, Rhodes, Le Bon, Moroder)
This plea for unity after what John Taylor has referred to as 'the divisiveness' of Donald Trump and Brexit definitely sounds like a Moroder track. The song lacks guitar – Dom Brown actually abandoned his instrument to sing backup when the track was played live – and the lyrics, including lines like 'If you wanna make a difference ... got to do it walking barefoot on the ground', ring a bit hollow. The band may have been reaching for a modern-day hit with this track, but sadly, it pales in comparison to the rest of the album.

'Wing' (Taylor, Taylor, Rhodes, Le Bon, Coxon, Ronson)
The album gets back on track with this ballad co-written by Ronson, who, along with Coxon, also plays guitar on the song. It opens with a riff reminiscent of a Bond theme song and features darkly gorgeous lyrics that evoke an internal struggle. Images such as 'a hungry demi-god' and a 'rabid dog at communion' appear to be metaphors for jealousy that eats away at the narrator, who longs for 'a wing of innocence [to] fly me out of here. Surrendered faith but I'm holding dread for a better man to be in my head'. The singer has stated that his words were inspired by a passage about jealousy in the book *The City Of Bohane* by Kevin Barry – and his performance is his best on the album.

'Nothing Less' (Taylor, Taylor, Rhodes, Le Bon, Alkan)
A series of strong tracks continues with 'Nothing Less', which features Saffron Le Bon on backup vocals and a vaguely Middle Eastern flair. The song includes more Bond-esque guitar from Coxon and harks back a bit to the *Big Thing* era, both musically and lyrically. The song begins with arty, cryptic lyrics – 'paved Nirvana, romance on the phone' – before Le Bon poses the profound questions, 'Does it even matter if we make it to the end? If we're carved in living rock, or just lines drawn in the sand?'

He wrote the tender lyrics for Yasmin Le Bon. "I want to thank you for all the nothings' – the things that didn't happen as well as the things that did', Le Bon told *Classic Pop* in 2021.

'Laughing Boy' (Taylor, Taylor, Rhodes, Le Bon, Coxon)
This song, which was released digitally in February 2022 to promote the deluxe edition of the album, brings to mind some of the band's early B-sides. The track includes delightful new wave-style synths and standout bass and really takes off with a chorus that's vintage Duran Duran. The lyrics – including 'the Palace Gang's back to old things. That's my cue, I'm getting out in style' – are about growing up and leaving behind the role of sidekick in a friendship, Le Bon has said.

'Hammerhead' (Taylor, Taylor, Rhodes, Le Bon, Alkan, Vanessa Mahi, Christopher Layton, Lei Jennings)
This unexpected highlight on the album features a brief yet subtle rap by Mahi (aka 'Ivorian Doll') and funky bass. The track could have been a contender to be the album's dud, but all players lift it to another level. It opens with an understated guitar riff before Le Bon's vocals kick in. The female backup vocals give the chorus a gospel feel, which, along with the mid-tempo groove of the verse and the UK drill rap in the bridge, make for an unlikely combination.

Le Bon, in his lyrics – including oblique lines like 'Good nights shanghaied bikinis aflame' – again addresses relationships and self-reflection, suggesting that the song isn't really about the titular shark. 'In the name of all the women I've known', he sings. 'The woman inside of me is out to take me down'. It's an audacious track that probably shouldn't work because of its diverse mix of musical styles, but does.

'Invocation' (Taylor, Taylor, Rhodes, Le Bon, Alkan, Coxon)
This song, a continuation of 'Hammerhead', uses the prior track's synth outro throughout and includes a Turkish-inflected guitar riff. Le Bon has said that his vocals were inspired by Bowie's 'Wild Is The Wind', and the two songs are musically similar, too, especially considering the dominant guitar riff on the *Station To Station* track. A definition of 'Invocation' is 'a formula for calling forth spirits' – and one can imagine that the ghostly meaning was Duran Duran's intention, especially given the darker direction they took with their next album.

'More Joy!' (Taylor, Taylor, Rhodes, Le Bon, Alkan, Coxon)
This track features just a sprinkle of Chai's joyful chants, cryptic lyrics, effects-laden guitar and synths that sound like they're being played on a Casio keyboard – or pulled from the soundtrack of a vintage video game. In stream-of-consciousness lyrics, Le Bon sings, 'Rorschach clowns. A smudge in the grey. Frantic we swim in a TV power game'. The song really takes off in the chorus, as each of Le Bon's lines is punctuated by Chai's chants of the track's title, followed by Coxon's guitar, which sounds almost like a chugging train.

The lyric video for the song, directed and animated by Melissa Ladybug, shows a male and female character and a dragon on a 'mystery train' ride through an anime wonderland. They arrive at their destination: a concert featuring an animated Duran Duran and Chai playing in a temple. It's a cute, colourful, fun clip for a shiny, happy song.

'Falling' (Taylor, Taylor, Rhodes, Le Bon)
This dreamy ballad features the unusual combination of funky bass and Garson's jazzy piano. Even though the eclectic song doesn't quite live up to the quality of the others on the album, especially given its role as the closing

track on such a strong LP, it's still a pleasant listen. Le Bon sounds fantastic, especially toward the end, when he reaches a higher register and is accompanied by additional noodling from Garson.

Extra Tracks

'Five Years' (Bowie)

Released as a single in January 2021

This track, which was released as a single months prior to the album's release and was included as a bonus track on the Japanese version of the LP, is the latest of several Bowie songs recorded by the band. It features Bowie pianist Garson and soulful backup vocals by Anna Ross and Barli. The song, about an impending disaster set to end the world in five years' time, was an appropriate choice of cover, especially amid the COVID-19 pandemic. As on all the band's Bowie covers, their reverence for The Thin White Duke is clearly heard, from Le Bon's powerful vocals to the inclusion of both a string section and his long-time pianist. Rhodes has said that Garson recommended that they perform the song, which had an added significance five years after Bowie's death.

The video, directed by Duran Duran videographer Gavin Elder, features a performance by the band, Garson, Ross, Barli and a string section as colourful imagery – 'painted' using virtual reality – swirls around them. The players were shot individually in London and Los Angeles, and the clip was put together using virtual reality. The video was the first of several by the band to use emerging technology instead of expensive on-location shoots, an approach enabling them to release several promotional clips for each new album.

Danse Macabre (2023)

Personnel:
Simon Le Bon: vocals
Nick Rhodes: keyboards
John Taylor: bass, guitar
Roger Taylor: drums
Additional musicians:
Andy Taylor: guitars, engineering
Warren Cuccurullo: guitars
Nile Rodgers: guitars
Dom Brown: guitars
Josh Blair: guitars
Victoria De Angelis: bass, vocals
Simon Willescroft: saxophone
Johnny Thirkell: flugelhorn
Anna Ross: vocals
Rachael O'Connor: vocals
Alexandra Stama: vocals
Recorded at Tape Modern Studios from 2022 to 2023
Produced by Duran Duran, Nile Rodgers, Mr Hudson and Josh Blair
Engineer: Josh Blair
Record label: BMG/Tape Modern
Release date: October 2023
Chart places: UK: 4, US: 57
Running time: 61:00 (De Luxe edition)
Current edition: 2024 BMG CD/LP

Future Past was well-received and marked a new era for the band: 40 years and counting into their career, they were about to receive their biggest honour and enter one of their most prolific periods.

Just four months after the album's release, Duran Duran received a nomination for the Rock & Roll Hall of Fame – their first. They had been passed over despite being eligible for induction for more than 15 years, but it appeared that the institution's opinion of the band had changed over time. It didn't hurt that MTV co-founder John Sykes was now the hall's chairman and that Le Bon and Taylor had forged a relationship with the institution when they inducted Roxy Music three years prior.

Duranies were elated and soon propelled the band to the top of the fan vote. Even though that tally accounted for little in the overall voting scheme, most artists who had won the fan vote in past years had been inducted. Duran Duran finished with over 930,000 votes – a whopping 250,000 more than the second-place finisher, rapper Eminem.

The band members were excited, too, and made plans to perform at the ceremony with Andy Taylor, who, along with Cuccurullo, was also being inducted. Ahead of the event, Duran Duran were seemingly everywhere. Their new concert film, *Duran Duran: A Hollywood High*, focusing on their ties to Los Angeles, played in select theatres worldwide, and they graced the cover of a special edition of *Life* magazine, which was available in shops throughout the US.

When the big day arrived, they opened the show, which was also held in LA. Oscar-winning actor Robert Downey Jr. gave their induction speech before the band took the stage, performing 'Girls On Film', 'Hungry Like The Wolf' and 'Ordinary World'. But Taylor was notably absent during the performance, as was Cuccurullo, who had never officially confirmed plans to attend. A subsequent message from Taylor sent shockwaves throughout the ceremony and the Duranie community. Le Bon read Taylor's heartfelt letter onstage, sharing the sombre news: the guitarist had Stage 4 metastatic prostate cancer and had suffered a setback that prevented him from attending the event. As Le Bon read from Taylor's message during the band's acceptance speech:

> Many families have experienced the slow burn of this disease, and of course, we are no different; so, I speak from the perspective of a family man, but with profound humility to the band, the greatest fans a group could have and this exceptional accolade … I'm so very proud of these four brothers, I'm amazed at their durability and I'm overjoyed at accepting this award. I often doubted the day would come. I'm sure as hell glad I'm around to see the day.

The announcement that Taylor had been privately ill for years cast a pall over the ceremony, but there was some good news to come of it. Taylor, who in his letter alluded to being treated by 'the Rodgers and Edwards of doctors', was still suffering from a disease that had no cure. But after the induction ceremony, scientist Sir Christopher Evans reached out to him with an offer of a groundbreaking treatment, Lutetium-177, which could extend his life by another five years. Taylor readied a new solo album, *Man's A Wolf To Man*, and the band announced that he would take part in their next project.

The idea for the new album was sparked by their Halloween show in Las Vegas prior to their Rock Hall induction. They played a mix of Halloween-inspired covers, as well as their own songs that fitted the theme, while wearing costumes – Le Bon even donned a wedding dress for the encore. Soon, the band returned to the studio. They had recorded versions of the songs they had played live but now expanded on the concept. They worked with Nile Rodgers, Mr Hudson and Josh Blair, and Le Bon flew to 'The Hotel Andy Taylor' on the Spanish island of Ibiza to record with the guitarist, who said that the singer had insisted that the band help pay for his medical care. Taylor told *The Daily Express* in 2023:

> We'd always maintained a gentlemanly approach to each other after I left. Verbally, we used to kill each other. The Gallaghers had nothing on us, but we all respected the boundaries and agreed we shouldn't publicly air any grievances. When I got to a point of needing the band, man, they were there.

Bob Clearmountain, who had mixed an unused version of 'Is There Something I Should Know?' back in the day and whom the band reconnected with at the Rock Hall induction, was brought on to mix the new album. Cuccurullo returned to the fold as well.

Le Bon called the new project 'spontaneous' – and it soon appeared that the band would conjure up a new album less than two years after their last. They recorded the LP in roughly three months – their fastest working pace since their debut album. The initial release of *Danse Macabre* included three new songs – 'Black Moonlight' with Rodgers, as well as the title track and 'Confession In The Afterlife' with Hudson. Le Bon described working with Rodgers on 'Black Moonlight' to *Forbes* in 2023:

> It was basically the first thing we did together. And we said, 'Oh, do you think we should sort of try and do something else?' He went, 'No. This is really good. So many times, we throw away the first things we come up with because we think we're going to find something better further along the line. This time, you've got something really good here.' So, we just followed it through.

The fast pace stood in contrast to the prolonged recording of the ill-fated covers album *Thank You*. The band again took on several cover songs, this time with confidence and maturity, working with their former guitarists despite past differences and finding room for other 'family and friends', both old and new. Touring members Dom Brown, Simon Willescroft and Anna Ross, as well as new backup singer Rachael O'Connor and Måneskin bassist Victoria De Angelis, were also invited on board.

Duran Duran had often explored sci-fi in the past – from naming the band after a character in *Barbarella* to the spacey synths on *Future Past* – but now they were sinking their teeth into the horror genre. Rhodes, being especially fond of Halloween, was the key force behind the project. But the other band members got into the spirit and – as always – were full contributors.

The album artwork was inspired by vintage séance pictures curated by Rhodes, with art direction and design by Rory McCartney. Patty Palazzo 'constructed' photos in which the band members appear to be taking part in the original séance, which Rhodes said was held in the UK in the 1940s.

Danse Macabre was released to general critical acclaim and became the band's third straight album to reach the top five in the UK. A year later, they released a *De Luxe* version. As with *Future Past*, the expanded edition included additional songs sprinkled throughout the tracklist instead of being tacked on at the end.

With *Danse Macabre* and their continued promotion of its theme – which has included *Secret Oktober*, a digital video release of the original Las Vegas show, as well as a sold-out concert at Madison Square Garden in New York the following year – Duran Duran are aiming to 'own Halloween', their manager said. After all, since their earliest days, they have always had 'a darker underbelly', Roger Taylor told *Forbes* in 2023, before rattling off three such songs, all from their debut album: 'To The Shore', 'Tel Aviv' and 'Night Boat'.

That Duran Duran have returned to the dark side more than four decades later makes perfect sense. They're just coming full circle.

'Masque Of The Pink Death' (Le Bon, Rhodes, Taylor, Taylor)
This instrumental, the first track on the *De Luxe* edition, establishes the mood for the Halloween party soundtrack that lies ahead. Its title is a nod to Edgar Allan Poe's *The Masque Of The Red Death*, and the music sounds like it could be played at a haunted house – or maybe a horror-themed speakeasy. It consists of Rhodes' eerie synths, John Taylor's solid bassline (which, at times, almost resembles the sound of knocking on a door), Roger Taylor's understated drumming and female backup vocals, setting the table for the main course to come.

'Nightboat' (Le Bon, Rhodes, Taylor, Taylor, Taylor)
Duran Duran revisit their moodiest song, '(Waiting For The) Night Boat' – titled 'Nightboat' here – with the guitarist from their classic lineup back to play his trademark slicing riffs. Le Bon's vocals have grown stronger with the passing years, and John Taylor's bass dances over the track, locking in with Roger Taylor's commanding drums. The new version of the classic from their debut album is slightly slower and more deliberate, with Rhodes' synths and Andy Taylor's guitar providing the most prominent links back to the original.

'Black Moonlight' (Le Bon, Rhodes, Taylor, Taylor, Rodgers)
Released as a single in October 2023
A 'zooming' sound effect opens this firecracker of a track, which was inspired in part by New York's Village Halloween Parade. Le Bon wastes no time as he launches into the verse, singing, 'Taken in possession by the music and beguiled'. Over less than three minutes, the band members put on a masterclass in synth pop. Both Rodgers – who co-produced the song with Blair – and Taylor deliver funky guitar riffs, John Taylor lays down a catchy bassline and Le Bon sounds fantastic. The single was dubbed a 'graveyard smash' by *Rolling Stone*.

The black-and-white video, for which the band reunited with 'Girl Panic' director Jonas Åkerlund, expands on the album artwork, showing the four members participating in a 'séance', complete with contorted bodies, bloodletting and Rhodes playing a theremin. The members unabashedly embrace the dark theme of the clip, which was filmed at the Chateau Marmont, a purportedly haunted hotel in West Hollywood where comedian John Belushi died.

'Love Voudou' (Le Bon, Rhodes, Taylor, Cuccurullo)
Cuccurullo returns on guitar for this reimagining of a track from *The Wedding Album*, mostly staying true to his original riffs. In this slightly sped-up version, Taylor mixes it up on bass, as does Le Bon with his vocals, and Roger Taylor adds an extra layer to the sound with the live percussion missing from the original. Also absent are the backup vocals of the late Lamya, though Ross and O'Connor do an admirable job here.

'Bury A Friend' (Billie Eilish, Finneas O'Connell)
This band's choice to cover this song by pop megastar Billie Eilish, written from the perspective of a monster under the bed, is unexpected but pays off. In their bold take on the quiet original, Le Bon adds an 'Eastern tonality' also used by the Australian band King Gizzard & the Lizard Wizard, which lends the main melody of the track a new and interesting element. Le Bon used a 'scale called hijaz kar, where you drop the second note and the sixth note, you flatten them', the singer told *Rolling Stone* in 2023. 'It suddenly changed the entire flavour of the song'. Andy Taylor, joined on guitar by co-producer Blair, adds his own fuzzy riffs.

'Supernature' (Marc Cerrone, Alain Wisniak, Lili-Marlene Premilovich)
Duran Duran take on disco, producing a better song than either of their tracks with Giorgio Moroder from *Future Past*, with their cover of Cerrone's UK top-ten hit, which features lyrics by new wave icon Lene Lovich (Premilovich). John and Roger Taylor lock in for a four-on-the-floor rhythm that's amped up from the original version, while Rhodes stays true to the Cerrone track by using many of the same sounds played on mostly analogue synths. With the addition of Rodgers' and Andy Taylor's disco-inflected guitar riffs and Le Bon's powerful vocals, they successfully reboot a well-known song in the classic lineup's style.

'Evil Woman' (Jeff Lynne)
Released as a single in October 2024
This synth-forward version of the Electric Light Orchestra hit is among the band's best covers but was unreleased until the *De Luxe* edition dropped. Duran Duran skip the iconic opening of the ELO classic, getting straight to business with their disco-fied version. Le Bon delivers his take on Lynne's vocals, using vibrato at times, and Brown adds an incendiary guitar solo.

The lyric video, by animation director Juan Pinto, envisions a Halloween party complete with dancing skeletons, disco balls, a blazing guitar and even ELO's 'Starlight' spaceship in the night sky.

'Danse Macabre' (Le Bon, Rhodes, Taylor, Taylor, McIldowie)
Released as a single in September 2023
The title track, a madcap 'dad rap', is one of Duran Duran's most inventive songs. Co-producer Hudson has called it both futuristic and ancient at the same time, an apt description given Le Bon's unique vocal delivery and Roger Taylor's shamanistic percussion. The rhythm-heavy track tells the tale of a wild Halloween party. It begins with a BBC sample of a foghorn at the Whitby Lighthouse – the 'Hawsker Mad Bull' mentioned in the lyrics. Cuccurullo's well-placed riffs add the doom and gloom, with an assist from his former bandmate John Taylor on guitar. Although the jury is still out on Le Bon's 'spoken-word' vocals, the song has a great chorus. 'Hey, no way, some ghost jive in a AC Cobra', he sings. 'Auto de Fé, get dirty up on the Danse Macabre'.

The video, produced using an AI animation program, is a vast improvement on the AI-directed clip for 'Invisible'. In it, a gothic Halloween party is attended by a cast of animated ghouls referenced in the song's lyrics – including 'nuns in the bed', a moaning 'Elvis' and 'a lone Natty Dread' – as well as the band members themselves.

'Secret Oktober 31st' (Le Bon, Rhodes, Taylor, Taylor, Taylor)
Duran Duran expand on their superb B-side, adding '31st' to the title and contributions from all five original members. The first 'Secret Oktober' featured only Le Bon and Rhodes. But on this version, John Taylor delivers a bassline worthy of the classic song and Andy Taylor finds room for his guitar riffs, all bookended by the sound of a wind-up music box. Whether this stately new version is better than the original is up for debate, as it lacks its DIY charm. But Le Bon's vocals are as good or better than on the original – and his 'Sh...' always elicits chills.

'Ghost Town' (Jerry Dammers)
Duran Duran deliver a cover that mostly stays true to the classic version with 'Ghost Town', a UK number-one originally by the Specials. In this fun iteration, Willescroft adds sax, joined by the flugelhorn famously heard on the original. John Taylor offers his take on the classic bassline, Andy Taylor contributes understated guitar and Ross and O'Connor seem to be having a blast with the iconic backup vocals.

'Paint It Black' (Mick Jagger, Keith Richards)
This cover of The Rolling Stones' song fits the Halloween theme, as well as the classic rock favoured on the *Thank You* album. The guitar riffs are right up Andy Taylor's alley, and Le Bon dials up the drama with his vocals, making changes to the melody and the meter of the words. (Notable tweaks from the original, which the band received approval for, include adding 'dead' before 'flowers and my love' and pluralising 'newborn baby'.) Covering The Stones

may not be an unexpected move, but Duran Duran are clearly having fun: what Halloween is all about.

The band's cover may be their way of saying thanks to The Stones' frontman after they heeded Mick Jagger's sage advice to 'stick together'; like The Stones, Duran Duran have shown remarkable endurance.

'Super Lonely Freak' (Le Bon, Rhodes, Taylor, Taylor, Taylor, Rick James, Alonzo Miller)

This track unites the band's own 'Lonely In Your Nightmare' with Rick James' smash 'Super Freak'. The two songs have similar basslines, so this version is rightfully bass-forward, but Taylor's classic fretless bass line from the *Rio* album track leaves little room for improvement. Midway through the song, the band members launch into James' party anthem, capped with a sax solo by Willescroft. The choice to cover the James hit is a natural one for Duran Duran, the band 'designed to make you party'. But aside from the basslines, the songs don't naturally fit together, so the musicians' exuberance is the only thing that makes this mash-up work.

'New Moon (Dark Phase)' (Le Bon, Rhodes, Taylor, Taylor, Taylor)

This track, another addition to the *De Luxe* edition, features Taylor's delightful take on his original bassline and some classic Andy Taylor guitar riffs. However, it's mainly a showcase for Le Bon's more mature vocal style. The singer was keen to redo the vocals on some of the band's old songs, and on this version of their early single, he ends the line 'as if I could ever hide' with a questionable vocal inflection. Although it's good to hear them revisit a song they mostly ignored for years, the new version lacks some of the energy of the anthemic original.

'Spellbound' (Susan Ballion, Peter Edward Clarke, John McGeoch, Steven Severin)

The album picks up the pace with this reverential version of a classic by Siouxsie and the Banshees, one of Duran Duran's favourite bands. The members are at their best on the post-punk anthem, as John Taylor delivers a driving bassline and Andy Taylor does an admirable job of replicating McGeoch's masterful guitar work. Le Bon – who often wears a Punk Masters 'Queen Sioux' shirt onstage that bears an image of the goth icon – stays true to her powerful vocals. He's joined by Ross and O'Connor, for whom he contributed excellent vocal arrangements on this song and throughout the album. 'Following the footsteps of a rag doll dance. We are entranced', Le Bon sings, adding his own flourish: 'Dance! Dance! Dance!'

'Psycho Killer' (David Byrne, Chris Frantz, Tina Weymouth)

Duran Duran offer yet another delightful take on a classic, and this time, Le Bon's vocals arguably sound better than on the original. His dramatic delivery suggests that, unlike Byrne, he's not inside the mind of a serial killer but perhaps in fear of him. Their cover features funky guitar from John Taylor and Brown, Rhodes' *Psycho*-esque keyboard stabs and dual bass by Taylor and De Angelis, who united over their admiration for Weymouth after meeting at a party. But Le Bon is the star of this show, emotively singing the famous French lyrics in the bridge, followed by the original song's memorable lines: 'We are vain and we are blind. I hate people when they're not polite'.

The 'visualiser' video, directed by Steven Merkens, consists of a brief piece of animation that repeats over the course of the song. The clip seems to be effective, as its YouTube views have far eclipsed those received by the proper video for 'Black Moonlight'.

'Confession In The Afterlife' (Le Bon, Rhodes, Taylor, Taylor, McIldowie)
This track fits in with the themes of both Halloween and of a band revisiting their past. 'Confession In The Afterlife' – with Le Bon's soaring vocals and Rhodes' tonal synths – sounds like a lost Arcadia track. Indeed, Duran Duran performed the song live at their 2024 Halloween show at Madison Square Garden, followed by Arcadia's 'Missing'. Both songs are haunting ballads about loss and what may follow. Hudson, who co-produced 'Confession' with Blair, contributes guitar, Brown delivers a bluesy guitar solo and Taylor seemingly channels Mark Egan, whose fretless bass can be heard on the Arcadia project.

From embracing the dark themes of *Duran Duran* and Arcadia's *So Red The Rose* to rebooting often-overlooked classics like 'New Moon On Monday', *Danse Macabre* shows a band in a reflective mood – but still looking to have a good time.

Extra Tracks
'Spooky' (Brides Of Duracula) (Mike Shapiro, Harry Middlebrooks Jr., James Cobb, Buddy Buie)
Le Bon originally tried performing the vocals on this song – a bonus track on the vinyl box set along with the instrumentals 'The Visitor' and 'Dialogues Of The Dead', as well as 'Instructions For A Séance' (a spoken-word track by Rhodes) – before stepping aside to give O'Connor a chance to sing lead. She's joined by fellow 'Bride Of Duracula' Ross in Duran Duran's take on this Classics IV track, versions of which have also been recorded by Atlanta Rhythm Section and Dusty Springfield, who changed the gender in the lyrics, as heard on this cover. The performance highlights how deep the talent pool is in Duran Duran's touring band, which includes O'Connor, an Irish singer who was mentored by Kylie Minogue during her stint on *The Voice UK*.

Duran Duran Collections, Live Albums And More

In addition to 16 studio albums, Duran Duran have a number of compilations and live albums, though they also have a frustrating amount of unreleased material, and several rumoured releases have yet to surface.

Following the success of *Rio*, the band released *Carnival*, a remix EP with territory-specific tracklists in different countries. These remixes, including the band's early Night Versions and Carnival Remixes from their first two albums, were eventually united on *Carnival Rio!* (Rhino, 2023), a Record Store Day release. (Though Record Store Day releases are typically limited editions, they can often be found on the resale market.) Other early EPs available in various countries include *Nite Romantics* (Japan), *Night Versions* (Australia), *Tiger Tiger* (Japan), *Mixing* (Italy) and *Strange Behavior* (Italy and Japan).

Duran Duran have two platinum-selling best-of albums: *Decade* (EMI/Capitol, 1989), a 14-song collection that was accompanied by a video release, and *Greatest* (EMI/Capitol, 1998). *Greatest* includes the same 14 songs as *Decade*, plus 'New Moon On Monday' – which had been omitted from the prior hits package – as well as 1990s singles 'Ordinary World', 'Come Undone', 'Serious' and 'Electric Barbarella'. It was followed by a DVD release in 2003. Another best-of collection, *The Biggest And The Best* (Music Club Deluxe, 2012), which showcases their 1980s hits, was also released in the UK.

There are several official live recordings covering various eras of the band. *Live At Hammersmith '82!* (EMI, 2009), recorded during the third night of a three-night stand at Hammersmith Odeon in London, was released on CD and DVD and later on limited-edition gold vinyl. The concert film shows the young band at the height of their powers – and before the pressures of fame had caught up with them.

In contrast, *Arena* (EMI/Capitol, 1984), Duran Duran's first officially released live album, was recorded 'around the world' during their massive *Sing Blue Silver* tour less than two years later. It features nine live tracks and the single 'The Wild Boys', and charted at number four in the US and number six in the UK. The *Arena* release was accompanied by the films *Arena (An Absurd Notion)* and *As The Lights Go Down*, as well as the *Into The Arena* board game. *As The Lights Go Down* (Rhino/Parlophone, 2019) – which was recorded in Oakland, California, in 1984 – has also been released on vinyl for Record Store Day.

Thanksgiving Live (Mountain Man Records, 2017), a 'semi-official' release widely available at many record shops, captures the band during their time as a three-piece act in the late 1990s. The recording of their show in Orlando, Florida, on Thanksgiving Day 1997 has been released on CD and vinyl.

Live From London (Epic Records, 2005), Duran Duran's official live album from the reunion era, was recorded during the final two dates of a five-night stand of sold-out concerts at Wembley Arena in 2004. It has been released on CD and DVD. *The Encore Series* (Themusic.com, 2003), authorised recordings of seven live shows in Japan and the US in 2003, also features the reunion-era lineup on CD.

A Diamond In The Mind: Live 2011 (Eagle Records, 2012), recorded at Manchester Arena during the *All You Need Is Now* tour, has been released on CD, DVD, Blu-ray and limited-edition vinyl. Though it was recorded more than a decade ago, it offers a glimpse of the type of stage show one might expect from the present-day version of the band: the greatest hits plus a smattering of their newest material at the time. Highlights include two *All You Need Is Now* tracks: 'Before The Rain' – on which Le Bon warms up his voice post-vocal scare – and the sublime 'The Man Who Stole A Leopard'.

Budokan (Warner Bros., 2018), a live album released on vinyl for Record Store Day, captures the final show of the *Paper Gods* tour at Nippon Budokan in Tokyo in 2017. The show was apparently recorded on video as well but has never been officially released.

Other live concerts made available on DVD (or Blu-ray) include the David Lynch-directed *Unstaged* (2014), as well as *A Hollywood High* (2023). There's also the beloved tour documentary *Sing Blue Silver* (1984), which features concert footage.

Additional video releases from the 1980s were included on EMI's box set CD/DVD reissues of albums up through *Big Thing*. These include *Working For The Skin Trade* (1988) and *Big Thing Live* (2010). The documentary and video compilation *Extraordinary World* (1994) was originally released on laserdisc and VHS, but as with much of the band's other work from the early to mid-1990s, it sadly remains out of print.

After the band parted ways with EMI in the late 1990s, the record company released various collections on CD. Among them is *The Essential Collection* (EMI, 2000), which highlights songs from the first two albums, including select B-sides. *Essential Duran Duran (Night Versions)* (EMI, 1998) includes Night Versions and other remixes of songs spanning from 'Planet Earth' to 'The Wild Boys'. The two-disc *Strange Behaviour* (EMI, 1999) includes yet more remixes, this time from the early years up through *The Wedding Album* era. Two box sets of cardboard-sleeved CD singles – *The Singles 1981–1985* (EMI, 2003) and *The Singles 1986–1995* (EMI, 2004) – have also been released.

Warner, which reunited Duran Duran with much of their back catalogue via their recording contract with the band in 2015, re-released the first five studio albums on CD and vinyl in 2024. Even though these releases are only bare-bones versions, it was mind-boggling that there hadn't been current editions available of these classic albums until then.

Since the band signed their most recent contract with BMG, which included their post-1997 back catalogue, the label has re-released *Medazzaland*, *Pop Trash*, *Astronaut*, *Red Carpet Massacre* and *All You Need Is Now* on CD and vinyl. *Reportage*, the unreleased album with Andy Taylor, reportedly is part of the deal with BMG. Band members have teased a possible release, but this lost album has mostly remained shrouded in secrecy.

Then there's the matter of *Liberty*, *The Wedding Album* and *Thank You*. The latter two albums achieved platinum and gold status, respectively, but all remain out of print and in demand on vinyl. Though a re-release of *The Wedding Album* has been rumoured for years, regretfully, it doesn't seem to be a high priority for the band or their former record label.

No matter what comes to fruition, Duran Duran are likely to continue touring and releasing new music for the foreseeable future. As Le Bon told Rob Brydon on his *Brydon &* podcast in 2024:

> We love working, and making a new record is such an important part of keeping the band's fire alive, keeping the band's fire stoked. If we let that fire go out, the writing one, then when you go out on tour and you just play a load of old songs, it doesn't feel so good. I can imagine that if you haven't written an album for five or ten years, maybe – and we will be going for the next ten years, if we can stay alive, obviously – that if it's ten years since your last new music ... it's a feeling we don't like. We like to have something new when we go onstage.

Over nearly 45 years, Duran Duran have achieved so much that they can and should be able to release whatever music they wish. However, the recent quote from the singer – now Simon Le Bon, MBE, after receiving the royal honour in November 2024 for his services to music and charity – suggests that they don't intend to rest on their laurels. This is something they've never done – and the spontaneous spirit that currently drives the band suggests that there are more exciting developments in the years ahead.

The Police *on track*
Every album, every song

Peter Braidis
Paperback
128 pages
41 colour photographs
978-1-78952-158-0
£16.99
$22.95

Every album by this legendary and hugely successful 80s band.

Forming when punk was starting to become a force, The Police – led by drummer Stuart Copeland and singer/ bassist Sting - used this emerging new form of music to create a sound that was both fresh, energetic and sophisticated. An early incarnation with guitarist Henry Padovani ended when Andy Summers joined the band and, under the innovative management of Miles Copeland, The Police took on the world.

From 1978 to 1983, the band released five magnificent albums that took in rock, reggae, and world music. A succession of massive hit singles, including 'Message In A Bottle' and the classic and often misunderstood 'Every Breath You Take' also cemented their success. By 1983, they'd become arguably the biggest band in the world, but egos and arguments took their toll, and the group split in 1986. Sting would go on to massive solo success, but a reunion tour in the 2000s broke box office records and finally closed the door on the band.

This book details every song and album from the first single to the last, making it a comprehensive guide to the music of one of the greatest bands in music history, with sales of over 100 million worldwide.

Depeche Mode *on track*
Every album, every song

Brian J. Robb
Paperback
176 pages
41 colour photographs
978-1-78952-277-8
£15.99
$22.95

Every album and every song by this world-renowned electronic rock band.

For four decades, Depeche Mode dominated electronic music, from the naïve melodies of 1981's *Speak & Spell* through to 2023's *Memento Mori*. Through changing line-ups featuring Vince Clarke, Alan Wilder, and Andy Fletcher, singer Dave Gahan and main songwriter Martin Gore have been the band's core. Starting as teenagers and now in their 60s, they have survived worldwide fame, addictions to drink and drugs, and near-death experiences, while continuing to innovate as technology and the music business evolved.

An acclaimed live band, it is through their fifteen studio albums that Depeche Mode have best expressed themselves, from the industrial darkness of *Black Celebration* (1986) to their popular breakthroughs with *Music For the Masses* (1987) and *Violator* (1990) and the emotional upheaval of 1993's *Songs of Faith and Devotion*.

The band survived the chaotic fallout from that album and tour in the mid-1990s, with Gahan experiencing a near-fatal drug overdose, to regroup with *Ultra* (1997). They continued their explorations of love, death, sex, and politics on acclaimed albums *Playing the Angel* (2005), *Delta Machine* (2013), and *Spirit* (2016). Inducted into the Rock and Roll Hall of Fame in 2020, proven survivors Depeche Mode have their story told here in song-by-song detail.

On Track series

AC/DC – Chris Sutton 978-1-78952-307-2
Allman Brothers Band – Andrew Wild 978-1-78952-252-5
Tori Amos – Lisa Torem 978-1-78952-142-9
Aphex Twin – Beau Waddell 978-1-78952-267-9
Asia – Peter Braidis 978-1-78952-099-6
Badfinger – Robert Day-Webb 978-1-878952-176-4
Barclay James Harvest – Keith and Monica Domone 978-1-78952-067-5
Beck – Arthur Lizie 978-1-78952-258-7
The Beat, General Public, Fine Young Cannibals – Steve Parry 978-1-78952-274-7
The Beatles 1962-1996 – Alberto Bravin and Andrew Wild 978-1-78952-355-3
The Beatles Solo 1969-1980 – Andrew Wild 978-1-78952-030-9
Blue Oyster Cult – Jacob Holm-Lupo 978-1-78952-007-1
Blur – Matt Bishop 978-178952-164-1
Marc Bolan and T.Rex – Peter Gallagher 978-1-78952-124-5
David Bowie 1964 to 1982 – Carl Ewens 978-1-78952-324-9
David Bowie 1963 to 2016 – Don Klees 978-1-78952-351-5
Kate Bush – Bill Thomas 978-1-78952-097-2
The Byrds – Andy McArthur 978-1-78952-280-8
Camel – Hamish Kuzminski 978-1-78952-040-8
Captain Beefheart – Opher Goodwin 978-1-78952-235-8
Caravan – Andy Boot 978-1-78952-127-6
Cardiacs – Eric Benac 978-1-78952-131-3
Wendy Carlos – Mark Marrington 978-1-78952-331-7
The Carpenters – Paul Tornbohm 978-1-78952-301-0
Nick Cave and The Bad Seeds – Dominic Sanderson 978-1-78952-240-2
Eric Clapton Solo – Andrew Wild 978-1-78952-141-2
The Clash (revised edition) – Nick Assirati 978-1-78952-325-6
Elvis Costello and The Attractions – Georg Purvis 978-1-78952-129-0
Crosby, Stills and Nash – Andrew Wild 978-1-78952-039-2
Creedence Clearwater Revival – Tony Thompson 978-1-78952-237-2
Crowded House – Jon Magidsohn 978-1-78952-292-1
The Damned – Morgan Brown 978-1-78952-136-8
David Bowie 1964 to 1982 – Carl Ewens 978-1-78952-324-9
David Bowie 1964 to 1982 – Carl Ewens 978-1-78952-324-9
Deep Purple and Rainbow 1968-79 – Steve Pilkington 978-1-78952-002-6
Deep Purple from 1984 – Phil Kafcaloudes 978-1-78952-354-6
Depeche Mode – Brian J. Robb 978-1-78952-277-8
Dire Straits – Andrew Wild 978-1-78952-044-6
The Divine Comedy – Alan Draper 978-1-78952-308-9
The Doors – Tony Thompson 978-1-78952-137-5
Dream Theater – Jordan Blum 978-1-78952-050-7
Bob Dylan 1962-1970 – Opher Goodwin 978-1-78952-275-2
Eagles – John Van der Kiste 978-1-78952-260-0
Earth, Wind and Fire – Bud Wilkins 978-1-78952-272-3
Electric Light Orchestra – Barry Delve 978-1-78952-152-8
Emerson Lake and Palmer – Mike Goode 978-1-78952-000-2
Fairport Convention – Kevan Furbank 978-1-78952-051-4

Also available from Sonicbond

Peter Gabriel – Graeme Scarfe 978-1-78952-138-2
Genesis – Stuart MacFarlane 978-1-78952-005-7
Gentle Giant – Gary Steel 978-1-78952-058-3
Gong – Kevan Furbank 978-1-78952-082-8
Green Day – William E. Spevack 978-1-78952-261-7
Steve Hackett – Geoffrey Feakes 978-1-78952-098-9
Hall and Oates – Ian Abrahams 978-1-78952-167-2
Peter Hammill – Richard Rees Jones 978-1-78952-163-4
Roy Harper – Opher Goodwin 978-1-78952-130-6
Hawkwind (new edition) – Duncan Harris 978-1-78952-290-7
Jimi Hendrix – Emma Stott 978-1-78952-175-7
The Hollies – Andrew Darlington 978-1-78952-159-7
Horslips – Richard James 978-1-78952-263-1
The Human League and The Sheffield Scene – Andrew Darlington 978-1-78952-186-3
Humble Pie –Robert Day-Webb 978-1-78952-2761
Ian Hunter – G. Mick Smith 978-1-78952-304-1
The Incredible String Band – Tim Moon 978-1-78952-107-8
INXS – Manny Grillo 978-1-78952-302-7
Iron Maiden – Steve Pilkington 978-1-78952-061-3
Joe Jackson – Richard James 978-1-78952-189-4
The Jam – Stan Jeffries 978-1-78952-299-0
Jefferson Airplane – Richard Butterworth 978-1-78952-143-6
Jethro Tull – Jordan Blum 978-1-78952-016-3
J. Geils Band – James Romag 978-1-78952-332-4
Elton John in the 1970s – Peter Kearns 978-1-78952-034-7
Billy Joel – Lisa Torem 978-1-78952-183-2
Journey – Doug Thornton 978-1-78952-337-9
Judas Priest – John Tucker 978-1-78952-018-7
Kansas – Kevin Cummings 978-1-78952-057-6
Killing Joke – Nic Ransome 978-1-78952-273-0
The Kinks – Martin Hutchinson 978-1-78952-172-6
Korn – Matt Karpe 978-1-78952-153-5
Led Zeppelin – Steve Pilkington 978-1-78952-151-1
Level 42 – Matt Philips 978-1-78952-102-3
Little Feat – Georg Purvis – 978-1-78952-168-9
Magnum – Matthew Taylor – 978-1-78952-286-0
Aimee Mann – Jez Rowden 978-1-78952-036-1
Ralph McTell – Paul O. Jenkins 978-1-78952-294-5
Metallica – Barry Wood 978-1-78952-269-3
Joni Mitchell – Peter Kearns 978-1-78952-081-1
The Moody Blues – Geoffrey Feakes 978-1-78952-042-2
Motorhead – Duncan Harris 978-1-78952-173-3
Nektar – Scott Meze – 978-1-78952-257-0
New Order – Dennis Remmer – 978-1-78952-249-5
Nightwish – Simon McMurdo – 978-1-78952-270-9
Nirvana – William E. Spevack 978-1-78952-318-8
Laura Nyro – Philip Ward 978-1-78952-182-5
Oasis – Andrew Rooney 978-1-78952-300-3

Phil Ochs – Opher Goodwin 978-1-78952-326-3
Mike Oldfield – Ryan Yard 978-1-78952-060-6
Opeth – Jordan Blum 978-1-78-952-166-5
Pearl Jam – Ben L. Connor 978-1-78952-188-7
Tom Petty – Richard James 978-1-78952-128-3
Pink Floyd – Richard Butterworth 978-1-78952-242-6
The Police – Pete Braidis 978-1-78952-158-0
Porcupine Tree (Revised Edition) – Nick Holmes 978-1-78952-346-1
Procol Harum – Scott Meze 978-1-78952-315-7
Queen – Andrew Wild 978-1-78952-003-3
Radiohead – William Allen 978-1-78952-149-8
Gerry Rafferty – John Van der Kiste 978-1-78952-349-2
Rancid – Paul Matts 978-1-78952-187-0
Lou Reed 1972-1986 – Ethan Roy 978-1-78952-283-9
Renaissance – David Detmer 978-1-78952-062-0
REO Speedwagon – Jim Romag 978-1-78952-262-4
The Rolling Stones 1963-80 – Steve Pilkington 978-1-78952-017-0
Linda Ronstadt 1969-1989 – Daryl O. Lawrence 987-1-78952-293-8
Roxy Music – Michael Kulikowski 978-1-78952-335-5
Rush 1973 to 1982 – Richard James 978-1-78952-338-6
Sensational Alex Harvey Band – Peter Gallagher 978-1-7952-289-1
The Small Faces and The Faces – Andrew Darlington 978-1-78952-316-4
The Smashing Pumpkins – Matt Karpe 978-1-7952-291-4
The Smiths and Morrissey – Tommy Gunnarsson 978-1-78952-140-5
Soft Machine – Scott Meze 978-1078952-271-6
Sparks 1969-1979 – Chris Sutton 978-1-78952-279-2
Spirit – Rev. Keith A. Gordon – 978-1-78952- 248-8
Stackridge – Alan Draper 978-1-78952-232-7
Status Quo the Frantic Four Years – Richard James 978-1-78952-160-3
Steely Dan – Jez Rowden 978-1-78952-043-9
The Stranglers – Martin Hutchinson 978-1-78952-323-2
Talk Talk – Gary Steel 978-1-78952-284-6
Talking Heads – David Starkey 978-178952-353-9
Tears For Fears – Paul Clark – 978-178952-238-9
Thin Lizzy – Graeme Stroud 978-1-78952-064-4
Tool – Matt Karpe 978-1-78952-234-1
Toto – Jacob Holm-Lupo 978-1-78952-019-4
U2 – Eoghan Lyng 978-1-78952-078-1
UFO – Richard James 978-1-78952-073-6
Ultravox – Brian J. Robb 978-1-78952-330-0
Van Der Graaf Generator – Dan Coffey 978-1-78952-031-6
Van Halen – Morgan Brown – 9781-78952-256-3
Suzanne Vega – Lisa Torem 978-1-78952-281-5
Jack White And The White Stripes – Ben L. Connor 978-1-78952-303-4
The Who – Geoffrey Feakes 978-1-78952-076-7
Roy Wood and the Move – James R Turner 978-1-78952-008-8
Yes (new edition) – Stephen Lambe 978-1-78952-282-2
Neil Young 1963 to 1970 – Oper Goodwin 978-1-78952-298-3

Frank Zappa 1966 to 1979 – Eric Benac 978-1-78952-033-0
Warren Zevon – Peter Gallagher 978-1-78952-170-2
The Zombies – Emma Stott 978-1-78952-297-6
10CC – Peter Kearns 978-1-78952-054-5

Decades Series

The Bee Gees in the 1960s – Andrew Mon Hughes et al 978-1-78952-148-1
The Bee Gees in the 1970s – Andrew Mon Hughes et al 978-1-78952-179-5
Black Sabbath in the 1970s – Chris Sutton 978-1-78952-171-9
Britpop – Peter Richard Adams and Matt Pooler 978-1-78952-169-6
Phil Collins in the 1980s – Andrew Wild 978-1-78952-185-6
Alice Cooper in the 1970s – Chris Sutton 978-1-78952-104-7
Alice Cooper in the 1980s – Chris Sutton 978-1-78952-259-4
Curved Air in the 1970s – Laura Shenton 978-1-78952-069-9
Donovan in the 1960s – Jeff Fitzgerald 978-1-78952-233-4
Bob Dylan in the 1980s – Don Klees 978-1-78952-157-3
Brian Eno in the 1970s – Gary Parsons 978-1-78952-239-6
Faith No More in the 1990s – Matt Karpe 978-1-78952-250-1
Fleetwood Mac in the 1970s – Andrew Wild 978-1-78952-105-4
Fleetwood Mac in the 1980s – Don Klees 978-178952-254-9
Focus in the 1970s – Stephen Lambe 978-1-78952-079-8
Free and Bad Company in the 1970s – John Van der Kiste 978-1-78952-178-8
Genesis in the 1970s – Bill Thomas 978178952-146-7
George Harrison in the 1970s – Eoghan Lyng 978-1-78952-174-0
Kiss in the 1970s – Peter Gallagher 978-1-78952-246-4
Manfred Mann's Earth Band in the 1970s – John Van der Kiste 978178952-243-3
Marillion in the 1980s – Nathaniel Webb 978-1-78952-065-1
Van Morrison in the 1970s – Peter Childs – 978-1-78952-241-9
Mott the Hoople & Ian Hunter in the 1970s – John Van der Kiste 978-1-78-952-162-7
Pink Floyd In The 1970s – Georg Purvis 978-1-78952-072-9
Suzi Quatro in the 1970s – Darren Johnson 978-1-78952-236-5
Queen in the 1970s – James Griffiths 978-1-78952-265-5
Roxy Music in the 1970s – Dave Thompson 978-1-78952-180-1
Slade in the 1970s – Darren Johnson 978-1-78952-268-6
Status Quo in the 1980s – Greg Harper 978-1-78952-244-0
Tangerine Dream in the 1970s – Stephen Palmer 978-1-78952-161-0
The Sweet in the 1970s – Darren Johnson 978-1-78952-139-9
Uriah Heep in the 1970s – Steve Pilkington 978-1-78952-103-0
Van der Graaf Generator in the 1970s – Steve Pilkington 978-1-78952-245-7
Rick Wakeman in the 1970s – Geoffrey Feakes 978-1-78952-264-8
Yes in the 1980s – Stephen Lambe with David Watkinson 978-1-78952-125-2

Rock Classics Series

90125 by Yes – Stephen Lambe 978-1-78952-329-4
Bat Out Of Hell by Meatloaf – Geoffrey Feakes 978-1-78952-320-1
Bringing It All Back Home by Bob Dylan – Opher Goodwin 978-1-78952-314-0
Californication by Red Hot Chili Peppers - Matt Karpe 978-1-78952-348-5
Crime Of The Century by Supertramp – Steve Pilkington 978-1-78952-327-0
The Dreaming by Kate Bush – Peter Kearns 978-1-78952-341-6
Let It Bleed by The Rolling Stones – John Van der Kiste 978-1-78952-309-6

Pawn Hearts by Van Der Graaf Generator – Paolo Carnelli 978-1-78952-357-7
Purple Rain by Prince – Matt Karpe 978-1-78952-322-5
The White Album by The Beatles – Opher Goodwin 978-1-78952-333-1

On Screen Series

Carry On… – Stephen Lambe 978-1-78952-004-0
David Cronenberg – Patrick Chapman 978-1-78952-071-2
Doctor Who: The David Tennant Years – Jamie Hailstone 978-1-78952-066-8
James Bond – Andrew Wild 978-1-78952-010-1
Monty Python – Steve Pilkington 978-1-78952-047-7
Seinfeld Seasons 1 to 5 – Stephen Lambe 978-1-78952-012-5

Other Books

1967: A Year In Psychedelic Rock 978-1-78952-155-9
1970: A Year In Rock – John Van der Kiste 978-1-78952-147-4
1972: The Year Progressive Rock Ruled The World – Kevan Furbank 978-1-78952-288-4
1973: The Golden Year of Progressive Rock 978-1-78952-165-8
Eric Clapton Sessions – Andrew Wild 978-1-78952-177-1
Dark Horse Records – Aaron Badgley 978-1-78952-287-7
Derek Taylor: For Your Radioactive Children – Andrew Darlington 978-1-78952-038-5
Ghosts – Journeys To Post-Pop – Matthew Restall 978-1-78952-334-8
The Golden Age of Easy Listening – Derek Taylor 978-1-78952-285-3
The Golden Road: The Recording History of The Grateful Dead – John Kilbride 978-1-78952-156-6
Hoggin' The Page – Groudhogs The Classic Years – Martyn Hanson 978-1-78952-343-0
Iggy and The Stooges On Stage 1967-1974 – Per Nilsen 978-1-78952-101-6
Jon Anderson and the Warriors – the Road to Yes – David Watkinson 978-1-78952-059-0
Magic: The David Paton Story – David Paton 978-1-78952-266-2
Misty: The Music of Johnny Mathis – Jakob Baekgaard 978-1-78952-247-1
Musical Guide To Red By King Crimson – Andrew Keeling 978-1-78952-321-8
Nu Metal: A Definitive Guide – Matt Karpe 978-1-78952-063-7
Philip Lynott – Renegade – Alan Byrne 978-1-78952-339-3
Remembering Live Aid – Andrew Wild 978-1-78952-328-7
Thank You For The Days - Fans Of The Kinks Share 60 Years of Stories – Ed. Chris Kocher 978-1-78952-342-3
The Sonicbond On Track Sampler – 978-1-78952-190-0
The Sonicbond Progressive Rock Sampler (Ebook only) – 978-1-78952-056-9
Tommy Bolin: In and Out of Deep Purple – Laura Shenton 978-1-78952-070-5
Maximum Darkness – Deke Leonard 978-1-78952-048-4
The Twang Dynasty – Deke Leonard 978-1-78952-049-1

… and many more to come!

www.ingramcontent.com/pod-product-compliance
Lightning Source LLC
LaVergne TN
LVHW030608040926
847199LV00033B/411

* 9 7 8 1 7 8 9 5 2 3 6 8 3 *